Praise for *Meet Their Needs, and They'll Succeed*

"Dr. Salome Thomas-EL's *Meet Their Needs, and They'll Succeed* is nothing short of extraordinary—a master class in leadership, vision, and the transformative power of education. During my tenure as a principal in Virginia, his 'Four Cs' were a guiding philosophy for me—the foundation for a nurturing and empowering culture. I am truly grateful to Principal EL for his dedication to young people and commitment to equipping educators with the tools to make a real difference. This book is a must-read for anyone committed to excellence in education."

> **—Dr. Diron T. Ford**, director of secondary instruction,
> Gloucester County (VA) Public Schools

"Are you looking for a book that keeps kids at the heart of decision-making? *Meet Their Needs, and They'll Succeed* is exactly what you need! With sincerity and passion, Principal EL offers a relatable and community-driven guide packed with actionable ideas schools can implement tomorrow. A must-read for anyone committed to empowering students and transforming school communities."

> **—Lauren M. Kaufman**, instructional coach, author, and speaker

"If you're looking for a book that will simultaneously tug at your heartstrings and uplift your spirit, this is it. In *Meet Their Needs, and They'll Succeed*, Principal EL shares the stories that compel his focus on the many paths that lead to student success. Organized in a clear and memorable structure, it's not just motivational; indeed, each chapter is laden with strategies, approaches, and examples that educators can put into place immediately. We have an obligation to do right by kids, and this book delivers. There are many reasons Principal EL chooses to stay, and we'd do well as a profession to follow his lead."

> **—Pete Hall**, administrator, education consultant, and co-author of *Relationship,*
> *Responsibility, and Regulation: Trauma-Invested Practices*
> *for Fostering Resilient Learners*

"In an era when people use schools as a social, political, and religious football, it is refreshing to read a book focused on the true purpose of education: serving children! Principal EL has produced a comprehensive book that will touch the hearts and minds of readers. It provides guidance for educators and for strategically engaging families and communities. Anyone truly interested in learning how schools can transform the lives of children needs to read this book."

> **—Anthony S. Muhammad, PhD,** author and educational consultant

"This book is a poignant reflection on the state of education, stressing the importance of creating a supportive and caring environment for all students. *Meet Their Needs, and They'll Succeed* acknowledges the heavy burdens placed on educators and advocates for systemic changes to address the widening achievement gap and other critical issues. Through rich stories and expertise gained over a long career serving school communities, Salome Thomas-EL issues a serious call to action for educational reform."

—**Abigail W. French**, career & technical education pathways coach, Frederick County (VA) Public Schools

"In my short career as a pro athlete in the NFL and long career as a high school and middle school teacher, I have always focused on being the educator and role model that my students needed. In his new book, *Meet Their Needs, and They'll Succeed*, Principal EL shares his "Four Cs" to help educators connect with their students and build brighter futures for our next generation. This is the right book for educators and administrators who need tools and strategies that work for all children. If we meet their needs, they *will* succeed."

—**Robert Jackson**, international speaker and award-winning author

"*Meet Their Needs, and They'll Succeed* is just the book we have been looking for in education. My own life was saved by adults who embraced the challenge of developing connections with struggling students like me, and I have dedicated my work to highlighting the trauma and challenges young people face daily. If you are truly committed to shaping the persistence, resilience, and success of your students, then this book is a must-read for you."

—**Dr. Tommie Mabry**, national education consultant, speaker, and author

"In *Meet Their Needs, and They'll Succeed*, Principal EL has created a blueprint for teaching critical thinking skills and raising a new generation of problem solvers. I have learned so much from Dr. EL's books and recommend you read this one more than once."

—**Susan Polgar**, chess grand master, four-time Women's World Chess Champion, coach, and author

"As a former elementary principal and now a district leader, I know firsthand that student success starts with meeting their most fundamental of needs. Salome Thomas-EL's insights in *Meet Their Needs, and They'll Succeed* remind us that relationships, engagement, and resilience are the cornerstones of a thriving school culture. This book is a powerful guide for any educator looking to create meaningful connections and lasting impact in their classrooms and beyond."

—**Amber Teamann**, executive director of technology & innovation, Crandall (TX) Independent School District

"Principal EL has once again captured the essence of what transforms students' lives—relationships. *Meet Their Needs, and They'll Succeed* is a must-read for educators who believe curiosity, consistency, and a culture of love are the foundation for success. With practical insights and heartfelt stories, this book will inspire teachers and leaders to connect deeply with students and create schools where every child thrives."

—**Joseph Jones, EdD**, superintendent, Newcastle County (DE)
Vocational-Technical School District

"I love that Salome Thomas-EL begins this book with his 'Four Cs'—being *crazy* about kids, staying *curious* about their lives, being *consistent* adults who show up for them, and developing a *culture* of support where every student feels a sense of belonging. From the benefits of teaching critical thinking skills to the how and why of establishing after-school programs, this book covers everything that educators should know and do to establish a positive and caring school community."

—**Dr. T. J. Vari**, senior director of product strategy, MaiaLearning

"It's a full-circle moment when your former high school student becomes an inspirational colleague! When I first met Salome Thomas-EL, he was an energetic and curious adolescent with leadership potential. Already a major figure in the field of education, Principal EL has cemented that reputation with this new book, *Meet Their Needs, and They'll Succeed*. True to his belief in the intrinsic worth of every student, he shares classroom practices that can be utilized by neophytes and veteran teachers alike. Dr. Salome Thomas-EL offers us ways to walk the walk."

—**Marsha Rosenzweig Pincus**, educator, writer, and creative consultant

"Principal EL's new book, *Meet Their Needs, and They'll Succeed*, is a must-have for every education library. I know firsthand what impact Dr. Salome Thomas-EL's approach has had on student achievement and school improvement. I have seen the ideas in this book transform teaching, learning, and school culture. To that end, I recommend it with full confidence."

—**Marcus Jackson, EdD**, chief academic officer,
Lancaster (TX) Independent School District

"I've been learning from Salome Thomas-EL for over a decade through his books, speaking, and social media. But after reading *Meet Their Needs, and They'll Succeed*, I realized he still has so much more to offer. This book moved my heart and gave me so many new perspectives and ideas that I found myself immediately calling colleagues and friends and sharing with them what I was learning. This book should be in every educator's library. Period."

—**Todd Nesloney**, author, speaker, and director of culture and strategic leadership for the Texas Elementary Principals and Supervisors Association (TEPSA)

"As a longtime teacher and principal in Philadelphia, I was able to witness the impact of Principal EL's work. All leaders know that the relationships we develop are important to students and teachers. I am sure every superintendent and principal will want their teachers to own a copy of *Meet Their Needs, and They'll Succeed*."

—**Dr. Robin Cooper**, president and principal officer of Teamsters Local 502:
Commonwealth Association of School Administrators

"Principal EL has masterfully distilled the essence of effective school leadership into his 'Four Cs' for school success, providing a roadmap that is both inspiring and actionable. Grounded in practical strategies and enriched by powerful real-world stories, this book ignites the passion educators need to embrace their true calling. A must-read for anyone committed to shaping schools where every student, and educator, thrives."

—**Neil Gupta, EdD**, superintendent of Oakwood City (OH) Schools,
education leader, and speaker

"*Meet Their Needs, and They'll Succeed* is a game changer for educators everywhere. Principal EL has delivered a powerful student-centered approach that speaks directly to the issues today's learners face. This book is the blueprint for anyone pursuing a career in education and touches on a multitude of topics that are pertinent to providing the best education for all students. A must-read for those committed to serving and uplifting the next generation."

—**Marques Stewart**, community superintendent,
Hamilton County (TN) Schools

"Once I started reading *Meet Their Needs, and They'll Succeed*, I couldn't put it down. I felt like I was in the room with Principal EL as his stories and insights unfolded! Through those powerful stories from his career in teaching and leadership, Principal EL breaks down complex challenges into tangible, accessible strategies for any educator. He doesn't shy away from the tough topics—high-quality reading instruction, trauma-informed practices, critical thinking skills, and alignment to the work that truly matters. This book is a must-read for teachers and administrators looking for inspiration, practical guidance, and a renewed sense of purpose."

—**Jessica Cabeen**, award-winning principal,
author, speaker, and leadership coach

MEET
THEIR
NEEDS AND
THEY'LL
SUCCEED

Many ASCD members received
this book as a member benefit
upon its initial release.

Learn more at
www.ascd.org/memberbooks.

MEET THEIR NEEDS AND THEY'LL SUCCEED

Transforming Students' Lives Through Positive Relationships

SALOME THOMAS-EL

ascd

Arlington, Virginia USA

2111 Wilson Boulevard, #300 • Arlington, VA 22201 USA
Phone: 800-933-2723 or 703-578-9600
Website: www.ascd.org • Email: member@ascd.org
Author guidelines: www.ascd.org/write

Richard Culatta, *Chief Executive Officer;* Anthony Rebora, *Chief Content Officer;* Genny Ostertag, *Managing Director, Book Acquisitions & Editing;* Stephanie Bize, *Acquisitions Editor;* Mary Beth Nielsen, *Director, Book Editing;* Katie Martin, *Senior Editor;* Donald Ely for Three Ring Studio, *Graphic Designer;* Valerie Younkin, *Senior Production Designer;* Kelly Marshall, *Production Manager;* Shajuan Martin, *E-Publishing Specialist;* Christopher Logan, *Senior Production Specialist;* Kathryn Oliver, *Creative Project Manager*

PAPERBACK ISBN: 978-1-4166-3359-4   ASCD product #121003

PDF EBOOK ISBN: 978-1-4166-3360-0; see Books in Print for other formats.

Quantity discounts are available: email programteam@ascd.org or call 800-933-2723, ext. 5773, or 703-575-5773. For desk copies, go to www.ascd.org/deskcopy.

ASCD Member Book No. FY25-3 (Apr 2025 PSI+). ASCD Member Books mail to Premium (P), Select (S), and Institutional Plus (I+) members on this schedule: Jan, PSI+; Feb, P; Apr, PSI+; May, P; Jul, PSI+; Aug, P; Sep, PSI+; Nov, PSI+; Dec, P. For current details on membership, see www.ascd.org/membership.

Library of Congress Cataloging-in-Publication Data is available for this title.
Library of Congress Control Number: 2024059054

34 33 32 31 30 29 28 27 26 25   1 2 3 4 5 6 7 8 9 10 11 12

This book is dedicated to my mom, Amena
(rest in peace), who was my first teacher, and
to all the teachers and administrators in the
world who are bringing joy to their schools and
giving children what they need each day.

MEET THEIR NEEDS AND THEY'LL SUCCEED

Foreword *by Baruti K. Kafele* xiii

Introduction 1

1. The Four Cs of Student Success 11

2. Trauma-Informed Practice 41

3. Engaging, Challenging, and Joyful Classrooms 55

4. Critical Thinking Skills 74

5. After-School Programs and Community Engagement 89

6. Educators Who Choose to Stay 108

Acknowledgments 125

References 127

Index 132

About the Author 139

Foreword

The first school leadership conference I ever attended was in the summer of 2003 at Fordham University in New York City. I was going into my fifth year of principal leadership in New Jersey, but this conference was a completely new experience for me. Every morning, all the principals would assemble in a general session before heading to breakouts.

As a Black man, I admit to always looking to see if there are other Black men present in the professional spaces I find myself in, particularly because Black men are such a small minority in the principalship. In the first general session, there were a few other Black men present. All the way across the room, I saw one with a familiar face. I had never met this person, but I recognized him because he had a book out, which I had read, called *I Choose to Stay*. I thought to myself, "That's Salome Thomas-EL." He had written the book while still a classroom teacher, just like I had done with my first book. After the session, I introduced myself, and we have been great friends and comrades in this work for more than 20 years now.

Lots of additional parallels between us have since come to light, including our support for positive school culture and engaging classrooms and our efforts to encourage educators to wrap their arms around students dealing with trauma. We have both gotten ourselves into "good trouble" in our respective school districts—not for doing anything wrong or incorrectly, but because of our staunch advocacy for our students and staff. This level of commitment might be why we are both known mostly by our professional titles: he's "Principal EL," and I'm "Principal Kafele." As education leaders, we both stand on our principles, despite the consequences, because we both recognize just how high the stakes are. It's no wonder we're so often mistaken for each other.

Throughout my career, I've preached from the hilltops that building strong relationships with students is the key to educators creating positive school cultures, and that positive school cultures are our best bet for transforming education. That's why I'm particularly excited about this book. Over the years, I've seen the impact of Principal EL's Four Cs philosophy: how it guides his work and how it benefits students, teachers, staff, and communities. This is on display in *Meet Their Needs, and They'll Succeed*. Salome's understanding of connection, joy, resilience, and engagement is widely known, and in these pages, he lays it all out in print in a way that's both inspirational and actionable.

As he and I both believe, curiosity, in combination with adopting innovative teaching strategies, is the key to reaching and empowering all students. And culture is the foundation for all this work. There are no optimal academic outcomes when the school's culture is counterproductive. Culture is a gateway to promoting critical thinking, boosting teacher and leader effectiveness, and increasing student academic performance. It is a direct reflection of the school's leadership and teachers. To that end, I anticipate this book, with its emphasis on the power of a relationship- and literacy-driven school culture, making a significant impact on those who choose to stay in our profession—and, through them, on the kids, families, and communities these educators serve.

—Baruti K. Kafele
Jersey City, New Jersey

Introduction

I could hear the door opening and closing, but I couldn't see anyone moving in the room. Then a nurse appeared from behind the curtain that circled my bed. "I'm sorry for waking you, Mr. Thomas-EL," the nurse said to me. "I'd like to apologize ahead of time. You'll get very little sleep tonight. The doctors want us to wake our patients every two hours to check their vitals, oxygen, and pain levels."

For the first time in my nearly 57 years on this earth, I was sleeping in a hospital bed—and on Father's Day, of all days! After experiencing stomach pain and chills all day Saturday, I finally went to the emergency room on Sunday morning. I had thought the doctor might tell me I had COVID-19, because we were in the middle of a pandemic, but no: my appendix had burst, and I needed immediate surgery. So, here I was, successfully down an appendix and being woken up every two hours by a nurse asking me questions about my life to distract me from painful things required to get fluids and medicine into my body.

"So what do you do for a living, Mr. Thomas-EL?"

I was tired and wanted to sleep, so I just told her I was a school principal in Wilmington, Delaware. She would be OK with this little snippet of small talk, right?

Nope! She wasn't.

"Wow, that's amazing!" my nurse exclaimed. "How are the kids?"

Now what could I do? I had to tell her the whole story about our wonderful students, teachers, and staff. About our national champion chess

1

program and my earlier career working in Philadelphia schools. She wanted to know if I liked my job. I told her that I absolutely loved it. "It's hard work, but it's God's work," I said, groggily doing my best to make conversation in the middle of the night.

When I woke up the next morning, I wasn't as tired as the nurse said I'd be. She ended her shift and said goodbye, assuring me that the daytime nurses would take good care of me and that she would be back at 11:00 p.m. Candidly, those daytime nurses were not nearly as friendly, caring, or loving as she was, but I made it through the day.

When the nurse returned that evening, she rushed into my room, loudly calling out my name: "Principal EL!"

I thought I was in big trouble. Few people who don't know me well call me "Principal EL." She went on to explain how she had looked up our school's chess team online and found so much information about them—and about me as well. "You *conveniently* left out how you have been on Dr. Oz's TV show!" she reprimanded, "and that you write books and have met Will Smith! I called my family and said, 'Look who my patient is!'"

What stood out to me, then and now, was the way this nurse repeatedly expressed pride in the work I'd done for decades as a teacher and principal. At a time when I was physically near my worst, it felt good to hear someone say they appreciated the work of educators.

Now, you may be wondering what a burst appendix, a couple of nights in the hospital, and a kind-hearted nurse are doing here at the start of a book about education. You have every right to be confused, so I'll clear that right up: The way this nurse treated me while I was in pain and struggling me made me feel special, like I mattered to her, like I had an advocate looking out for me. It reminded me of what I wanted to do for all my students when I was a teacher, and it reminded me of what I expected from my teachers as a principal: to recognize all students' fundamental humanity as well as their specific individuality. To create a space that's engaging and joyful for kids in the middle of anything painful or challenging that might be going on in their lives outside our school.

Every student should feel that they matter and are important. If you can only remember one line from this book, it should be that. As educators, our goal each day should be to give our students what they need to succeed in school and in life. That means we must be prepared to reach out to them and meet them where *they* are, *as* they are. Yes, even though, initially, they may be as reluctant to engage as I was when my wonderful overnight nurse first reached out to me.

Now I just told you a story about *one* nurse who cared for me. But as you know, there are countless nurses all over the world caring for their patients. Yes, that story was about my struggle, but it was also about a nurse's success. She developed a positive relationship with her patient. She didn't care that it would be a short-term relationship and that we might not see each other again once I was discharged. She didn't allow my race, medical condition, or ethnicity to interfere with her belief that I could get better with her help. She succeeded in making that hospital room a place where I felt loved and cared for.

All good teachers, like nurses, want their students to feel this way in the classroom. But here's the problem: They don't have one or two patients in a room. Teachers must care for 20, 30, sometimes 40 students at once, with no privacy curtains or doors to close. They act as instructors but also as counselors, social workers, nurses, therapists, and, even, parents at times to those 20 or 30 students each day!

And all of this takes place surrounded by whatever else is going on in life, be it a pandemic, a nationwide movement for social justice, all our personal challenges, and an increasing achievement and equity gap in our nation's schools. Add to that the monthly school shootings, and it's easy to understand why so many teachers and administrators are leaving the profession. They fear for their health and safety. They feel exhausted, overlooked, and underappreciated.

As an educator, maybe a parent, and a member of the community, I am sure you are already aware how high the stakes are. Schools continue to be impacted by widening achievement gaps, poor funding, struggles with diversifying the teaching profession, recovering from the pandemic, and a myriad of safety and mental health issues. I often wonder how teachers and other educators are supposed to make a positive difference in student learning outcomes when there are so many barriers and the deck is stacked against them. Yet there is no more important time than now to seek true, meaningful reform in education.

I saw the need for change early in my teaching career, back when I was working in a Philadelphia school that primarily served students and families of color. At the time, though, I didn't know how to start a revolution or become a disruptor. I'm a product of the housing projects and public housing in North Philadelphia (the same community responsible for Dawn Staley, the Women's NCAA Basketball Championship–winning coach). I was raised by a single mom. I could relate to my students. But I still struggled to find ways to motivate them to engage with and value the lessons I was trying to teach them.

Until I introduced them to chess.

Chess helps students improve their confidence, resilience, and self-efficacy. When I started teaching students receiving special education services and with discipline issues, I realized most needed to develop critical thinking and problem-solving skills in order to make better decisions in school and life. They also faced significant daily challenges at home— from poverty and violence to neglect and low expectations. The older students got, the more their interest in school waned. I could see them beginning to lose hope.

Not all inner-city schools face these issues, nor are these challenges limited to urban areas. But inner-city, urban, and rural communities share characteristics quite different from suburban school districts, which—make no mistake—have their issues as well. All schools and districts do. And all students need educators who care enough to fight the good fight and never give up on them. All students deserve access to high-quality teachers who are prepared to meet their needs, school and district leaders who support teacher development, and the proper resources to help them succeed.

One of my biggest reasons for teaching chess to my inner-city students was that I wanted to find a great equalizer—an activity or game where the size or gender of the opponent did not matter. It was just a battle of minds. It didn't matter if you were big or small, loud or quiet. Whether you talked trash or were humble, you had to be ready on the chess board.

I remember working with two young ladies a few years ago: Destiny and Maddy. Both were filled with potential, but they were quiet and reserved and hung back in class. I was looking to engage them and open their eyes to their own power and possibility. Unlike many of their classmates and friends, Destiny and Maddy were not interested in the dance and cheerleading activities our school offered. Now, my own two daughters had been cheerleaders and dancers, so I understood and appreciated the value of those paths, but it was clear that Destiny and Maddy needed something different.

I firmly believe that active curiosity is the foundation of all learning. I had to be actively curious about who these students were and who they wanted to become. As it turned out, Destiny and Maddy both *loved* chess. They were two of the nicest young ladies I had ever met as elementary and middle school students, but on the chess board, you did *not* want to mess with them! As they continued playing the game, they became more vocal in class and active in school programs. They went on to help our middle school team win two national chess titles and graduated from the same high school one year apart: the Tower Hill School in Wilmington, Delaware. Today, Destiny is enrolled at Cornell University, and Maddy attends the University of Virginia. Both are thriving, two roses that grew from concrete. They are testimony to what is possible when schools spark teachers' curiosity about their students and students' curiosity about the world.

So, who is this book for? I wrote it for any educator with the desire to ensure all students have equitable access to

- Positive adult-child relationships;
- Engaging and challenging classrooms;
- A culture of literacy and high-level learning; and
- Other research-based and proven strategies that support student success.

I've written this book to support schools and districts in leading their students in a bold and different way. We need a new generation of courageous leaders who will step up to support and empower teachers and other staff members to inspire our young people to shine. Coaches, mentors, counselors, and advisors also play a major role in our youth's social and emotional development. It's time for every adult in the school and community to commit to serving our students by preparing them as best we can for the life and leadership roles that await them. In this book, we'll dig deep into the theories and practices proven to be effective.

First on the agenda is a discussion of the internal work educators must embrace to best serve all students. In **Chapter 1**, we'll explore my Four Cs of School Success:

- Crazy about our kids
- Curious about their lives outside school
- Consistent adults in students' lives
- Culture of love, support, and high expectations for all students

Every chapter addresses the foundation and root of what kids need and how these Four Cs impact their lives. I've given more than 500 talks on education, teaching, leadership, and parenting in the United States, Canada, the Caribbean, Europe, and Africa. No other topic gets the attention and responses—in person, virtually, or on social media—like my Four Cs of School Success!

After learning about the importance of the Four Cs, I'll take you on a journey in **Chapter 2** to analyze the positive power of having trauma-informed classrooms, staff members, and leaders. If we are to create high-quality learning environments that meet the social and emotional needs of our students, we must learn how to provide the right kinds of additional support for the growing number of students who experience trauma and adversity linked to poverty, homelessness, food insecurity, lack of healthcare, and so many other issues.

With this blueprint to guide us, we'll spend the remainder of the book considering what educators must do daily to best support all students. This is the work on the ground: the hustle and grind of teachers, staff members, and administrators, which most of the public rarely get to see in action.

Chapter 3 is probably one of the most important chapters I've ever written in a book, and this is book number six for me. I dive into how employing curricular and pedagogical practices that are engaging, challenging, and joyful can change the lives of young people. Don't miss the word *joy* in that last sentence! I truly believe that a school leader's most important job is to help make the school feel positive to kids, teachers, and staff. This is the secret to a successful learning environment. Of course, school safety, parental engagement, research-backed instructional practices, and so many other factors are important, too. But creating welcoming, positive, inclusive, equitable classrooms that feel joyful to the young people in them is a game-changer.

Chapter 3 also focuses on what is arguably *the* top priority for most schools and school districts in the United States: prioritizing literacy and reading across all content areas. Creating a culture of literacy requires a clear focus on literacy skills and their development. This focus must be shared by every adult in the building. To close the achievement gaps, students need to be immersed in literacy-rich environments, learn to read at an early age, and have effective supports available to them.

In the last section of Chapter 3, we explore how to increase student resilience by creating a growth mindset culture in every classroom. We need students to understand the value of hard work and feel free to be creative and take risks. Students must learn to accept their failures and use their mistakes as a springboard to future success. As educators and parents, we can't prevent young people from facing adversity, but we can teach them a constructive way to approach challenges and struggles.

In **Chapter 4**, I discuss the benefits of teaching critical thinking and how problem solving helps young people learn to deal with real-world issues and overcome obstacles. Life is about the decisions we make. Students who learn early on how to make better decisions and solve problems are well-equipped for life. I chose to use chess as a tool to reach students because it empowers reasoning, logic, patience, and critical thinking.

For many educators, **Chapter 5**, which covers developing after-school programs and engaging the community, will be compelling and impactful. Communities and schools benefit when students are engaged in high-quality after-school programs that foster a sense of belonging and provide productive learning time. Developing extracurricular programs that address the academic, social-emotional, and safety needs of all students is essential to the success of schools around the nation. These programs keep students safe during the afternoon and evening hours. They provide a way for educators to fine-tune instruction to accelerate learning, build and strengthen relationships with students, and help students access and grow their talents.

I also talk in Chapter 5 about engaging with the surrounding community. When families and community members are involved in schools, student achievement improves. Students and staff feel more confident about taking risks and facing challenges. We explore how to create strong family-school-community partnerships and initiatives that help support students and close gaps in achievement and equity.

Finally, **Chapter 6** is both our conclusion and our look-forward. Even before the COVID-19 pandemic, staying in the teaching profession wasn't easy, especially in inner-city and rural schools. The volume of demands, high-stakes testing, dwindling resources, student trauma, low pay, and other outside issues make teacher recruitment and retention an ongoing challenge. Couple these factors with the outside distractions, school violence, and the political battles fought over what should be taught in schools... the tea kettle is always boiling! A pandemic just turns up the heat even more. Thousands of teachers leave the profession each month, and we all understand why (Walker, 2022a).

But there are those who choose to stay, despite it all. Why is that? Are they unusually purpose-driven? Do they see teaching as an act of service? We will try to answer these questions in this crucial chapter. As you'll see, I believe an educator's impact is determined by their ability to *learn* as much as their ability to teach. They must be curious. Effective educators want to learn everything they can about giving students what they need to be successful. Our students will benefit from us all becoming learners in school with them.

Each chapter in this book closes with reflection questions, things to think about or do now, and some suggested longer-term actions to support all our classrooms and schools. The reason is simple: we must do the work necessary to build school cultures where students feel a sense of belonging... where they are positively engaged in the learning process, the curriculum, the school as a whole, and the greater community. The key to transforming education in the United States for the better is not focusing on test scores but on providing every student with the opportunity to find success. This work begins with developing meaningful relationships with our students.

In many ways, this book reflects my own journey as a student in a struggling community and school system, and as a teacher and leader in similar communities and schools. What you will find on these pages are the many positive stories and life lessons I have accumulated over the past 38 years. After reading this book, you won't just have a blueprint for creating joyful classrooms—you will be excited to start building. You will understand that reaching all kids is far more possible than it may seem.

Thanks for taking this journey with me. I promise you this book will be interesting (and joyful) and go way beyond asking you to change a few lessons or improve your bulletin boards. It will move you to become the change you want to see in your school and district. To make a choice to stay, even in these challenging times. Please read this book with an open heart and mind. I can't wait to hear your feedback.

1

The Four Cs of School Success

Early in my career, I resolved to be the educator who did *more* than just teach facts and convey information. I wanted to be a role model, a father figure, a mentor, and an example for my students. I suppose this was because I had a rough upbringing, lacking some basic necessities and essential family connections. I wanted to dedicate my career to making life just a little easier for kids with similar backgrounds. Not easy—just *easier*.

My priority was creating healthy, long-lasting connections and making school feel like a sanctuary for students. I wanted to enhance relationships rather than work to boost test scores and be an adult whom my students could rely on to help them succeed. I vowed to focus on building connections that would allow students to trust me. After all, trust is the foundation of healthy and sustained relationships, and students in schools where relationships and connections are authentic are more likely to be engaged in school and succeed academically (Creekmore & Creekmore, 2024).

Before long, however, I began to see patterns of tardiness, absenteeism, and lack of planning and organization in my students' behavior. This was far from the desired trajectory. Did I need to be "tougher" on them? With knowledge of how hard it was "out there in the real world," I began to tighten up my program, shifting to an approach built around the idea that they better buckle up and prepare for a bumpy road. "Get to school on time, and bring all the supplies needed for a successful day... or suffer the consequences." This was my message to them each day, and I was an absolute stickler about it, coming down really hard and tolerating no excuses—some of which were no doubt legitimate explanations of extenuating circumstances. Nope. To me, they were *all* excuses, and I was *not* having them.

Looking back, I realize how strange it was that I gave my students so little grace when I had been given so much. Just ask Marsha Pincus, my high school English teacher. As she has told audiences at speaking engagements of mine, I was frequently late to her class. From her classroom window, she used to watch me grabbing food from the neighborhood pretzel stand when I should have been in my seat. But Ms. Pincus never complained about or reported my tardiness because she knew my home circumstances and was sure I was hungry in the morning. I needed those pretzels! But *my* students? No. *They* needed to be in my class on time each day! How did I miss what Ms. Pincus and many other amazing teachers so acutely saw and compassionately acted upon?

I can still hear Dr. Deidre Farmbry, my former teacher and principal, telling me that how I treated students and colleagues would determine my path in education. *Be firm,* she told me, *but teach and lead with a loving heart.* Yet early in my career, no student was allowed in my classroom without a pencil or pen and a notebook. Even when I worked in our alternative program, In School Suspension (ISS), or "In House," as the kids often referred to it, I still required my students to meet all the demands of the other educational programs and classrooms in our school. I gave out very few extra pencils or lunches, and I rarely, if ever, issued extensions for students who didn't hand in assignments on time.

I can clearly picture three of the funniest students I ever had in ISS: Rodney, Shawn, and Dante. They were middle schoolers when I met them. Although they were all very smart, they were also unfocused and rarely came to school with the completed homework, school supplies, or the kind of attitude they needed to be successful in my classroom. Officially, all three were considered "at risk" and labeled as "struggling." So, did I give them the internal support that would have eased that struggle? I did not. What I did was push them even harder to abide by my rules. And instead of trusting me, which is what I wanted, they began to resist even more. Instead of learning about their lives outside school, building our relationship, and trying to deepen our connection, I drove their interest in school even lower.

To be honest, back then, success for Rodney, Shawn, and Dante seemed like an improbable outcome. I was in charge of ISS in those days, and they were in there with me regularly for various infractions like cutting class, disrespecting teachers and staff, and damaging school property. Let's just say they were repeat offenders. This was frustrating to me, and I wondered why I wasn't making an impact on them. Why did they keep getting referred back to ISS? I mean, they were there with me more than they were with their assigned teachers. Why wasn't I inspiring Rodney, Shawn, and Dante to want to stay in their designated classes and learn?

My breakthrough came when I began to pay more attention to these three young men and less attention to their infractions. Instead of doing all the talking, I began to listen to them—and to my other students, as well. I discovered not only the root of their challenges but also a lot about their strengths, interests, and gifts. This was a significant part of my transformation process. I realized that, like many students, these young men were only interested in learning when they believed the person leading the learning was truly invested in them.

As I continued building a relationship with Rodney, Shawn, and Dante, I discovered some of their anger was associated with the Rodney King situation, which was a hot news topic at the time. Rodney King was a young Black man in Los Angeles, California, whose brutal beating at the hands of LAPD officers was captured on camera; the footage led to civic unrest in Los Angeles and many major cities across the United States. Shawn, especially, vocalized his distrust for police officers and those in authority, and this caused discomfort for some of his teachers, many of whom (including me) had police officers in their families. After a few conversations with Shawn, I was able to see through the anger and notice his strong sense of social justice, which many young people in our schools share. By giving Shawn opportunities to share his passionate thoughts about this matter, I was able to redirect him to healthy discussion and behavior: positive activism instead of negative acting out.

From Shawn, I learned that being listened to, being heard, can be powerfully healing. I started creating opportunities to listen more. I started taking Shawn, Rodney, and Dante to basketball games. I brought them to lectures to hear nationally recognized speakers discuss race relations in America and entrepreneurship in the community. I brought them to visit college campuses. It didn't take long for a few young ladies in the school to become a part of our student mentoring group, and the guys were very respectful and welcoming. I was proud of them.

The relationship we all formed changed each one of them, and it changed me, too. I even invited Rodney, Shawn, and Dante's other teachers to come into ISS and observe the "different" students these three were in our program: how hard they worked, how much success they were finding. They were also able to have discussions about the trauma and struggles they faced outside school. Eventually, the young men went back to their assigned classes, and I saw less of them over time. Ultimately, Rodney, Dante, and Shawn grew from disenchanted, reactive young men with no real plans to committed students who worked with intention and mapped out their futures. They kept that momentum and were persistent enough to make it out of our struggling neighborhood and graduate from high school and college. Today, they are all loving and committed fathers, community members, teachers, mental health counselors, businessmen, and entrepreneurs. This is not a small feat by any means.

The outcome could have (and would have) been entirely different if the school's culture hadn't been one that supported educators being crazy about kids and working hard to identify and then provide what our students needed, starting with empathy and grace.

I started my new path as an educator by looking at my students differently and, yes, listening to them more. I had a new perspective. In my mind, I followed them home from school and back each day. I began asking students about their lives outside school, what was happening in their world, and how they felt. As I understood *them* differently, they understood *me* differently. I saw myself in them—in their struggles, their resilience; I wanted them to begin seeing themselves in me—their possibilities, their potential.

It was working. My struggling students started keeping their heads up more. There was more eye contact, and there were more smiles. Overall,

I saw more regular attendance, more engagement in schoolwork, and deeper connections between students and staff. I had hoped they would see the worth of developing a relationship with me, but I had underestimated just how powerfully making a connection with me would improve their trust in and ability to connect with other adults in our school. I even noticed more students hanging around after school and participating in extracurricular activities. When students are not rushing to get out of the building, you know you've created a culture where students feel like they've found a second home. This all planted the seed that grew into the Four Cs.

All About the Four Cs

I consider the Four Cs to be the critical elements of building the types of relationships our students need to begin to understand their great potential. They have driven my work in schools and classrooms over the past 38 years. I receive the most feedback whenever I share the Four Cs with audiences of thousands of educators around the world, and the Four Cs are consistently posted on Twitter (X), Facebook, Instagram, and other social media platforms.

Once I was able to connect my love for kids and teachers with concrete ways to support them both, I began to experience major shifts in the classroom and school culture. I believe the same will happen for other educators who embrace the Four Cs.

The Four Cs drive change, empower confidence, and transform culture. The shift we made in our school's culture was a result of a constant focus on the areas we knew would most impact student resilience and emotional well-being. These areas of focus became my Four Cs for school and classroom success:

- **C**razy about kids
- **C**urious about their lives outside school
- **C**onsistent adults in students' lives
- **C**ulture of love, support, and high expectations

Let's visualize it (see Figure 1.1).

FIGURE 1.1
The Four Cs

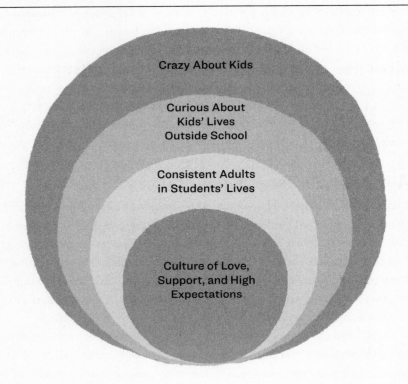

It all starts with being crazy about our kids—that's why it's got the most real estate in the figure. It means loving them before we ever meet them and committing to support them no matter what, regardless of their behavior, academic success, or status. This passion leads to curiosity—a spark that inspires us to learn not just about them as students but as individuals with lives outside school. And what we often learn is that the children who need the most love tend to ask for it in difficult ways and can be leery of accepting it at first. Being consistent adults—adults who show up regularly with this positive, curious energy—means we can set an example for our students. We show them they can rely on us, no matter what. And these attitudes and actions inform a surrounding culture of love and support. In this way, the Four Cs are a means to making a positive and lasting impact as a teacher, leader, and educator.

The remainder of this chapter will show you how to embrace and implement the Four Cs.

The First C: *Crazy About Kids*

Educators and parents often ask me what it means to be "crazy about kids." I still think a long time before I respond.

I begin with the easy stuff. "Crazy about kids" is all about positive emotions. I know some people use the word *crazy* in a derogatory way, like, "You've got to be crazy to go into the teaching profession" or "Kids these days are crazy." On the contrary, we are referring to becoming *ecstatic* about our students—elated for and about them.

Being crazy about the kids in your school is multifaceted, even though, at its essence, it's simple. It means more than just noticing that they seem down one day and caring if they are OK, and more than just making sure to call on them enough in class. Of course, those things are important, but our students—all of them, no exceptions—need what the amazing Dr. Rita Pierson (may she rest in peace) called a "champion and advocate."

Being crazy about kids isn't something you learn in college or your graduate education program. Moreover, it can't be acquired in our teacher and school leader preparation programs, which focus on all the basics of classroom- and school-level success: classroom management, leveling and managing reading groups, whole-class instruction, small-group instruction, technology-based interventions, and so on. Although it may be true that preparation and organization can yield well-run classrooms, those kinds of programs and courses can't teach you what it feels like to be crazy about kids. This comes from the heart. You can gain all the tools in the world from college and professional development programs, but what really fuels educators' ongoing commitment to the profession is our delight in kids themselves.

Therefore, "crazy about kids"—the first C, the foundational C—means exactly what it says. We should not just tolerate, not just like, but be absolutely *ecstatic* about the idea of our students, their presence, their promise, and their potential!

We should revel in our opportunity to help them live their best and most rewarding lives. We should help them feel emotionally and physically safe in school and do this by ensuring we give them what they need to succeed inside the classroom, at school, and out in the community. And we meet them where *they* are, not where *we* are.

The Four Cs are not a concrete or "one size fits all" approach but a set of concepts—a framework to guide you on your journey to positively affect students and their families. Each of the Four Cs is specifically chosen to allow you to embrace the mindset and attitude of the concept and apply it where needed in school. I have also provided a set of strategies to help you develop effective routines to focus your work around each of the concepts. The strategies provided are filled with tips and techniques to enable you to make an impact—not only to support the success of your students but also to create a joyful and engaging space for you all to share.

Strategy 1: Maintain the physical space in a way that promotes, strengthens, and supports the health and safety of all students and staff.

As a school leader, I focus my attention on the needs of my students, but I can't forget about the other people in the building who care for and support those students each day. Teacher well-being affects student well-being, along with the levels of learning, energy, and joy I want to see in our school. All of these begin with my leadership. Teachers who don't feel supported or cared for won't be excited to teach great lessons. Creating a safe and healthy environment benefits both staff and students. There have been numerous studies by the EPA on the impact the school environment has on child development, academic performance, and attendance. There is a strong relationship between classroom environment, school climate, and student achievement (U.S. Environmental Protection Agency, 2012). Creating this climate—one where teaching and learning flourish, and where everyone feels and actually is safe—requires deliberate action (DeWitt & Slade, 2014).

Here are some simple efforts that will make a noticeable impact. Note that they are generally the purview of a school leader.

- **Celebrate the contributions of your custodial team.** These valuable members of the school community must know how much they matter and that they are trusted to ensure the cleanliness of the school building and the expeditious completion of all repairs.

- **Verify that every system works as well as possible, whether the building is old or new.** This includes making sure all doors lock from the inside, all windows open and close properly, and the heat/air conditioning is working. If students and staff aren't warm enough on cold days and comfortably cool on hot days, it will be difficult for much teaching and learning to take place.

- **Confirm that all water fountains and bathrooms are working and cleaned regularly.** Kids may not always be good about keeping their bathroom at home clean, but they *will* let you know the moment their school bathroom needs to be cleaned or if there is no soap in the dispenser. Paper towels are a big issue, too. Provide them, even though kids may struggle to find the trash can. Hallways are a great place for posters and signs as reminders of their responsibility to leave bathrooms as clean as they found them.

Over the years, I have made many improvements in the schools where I've worked. Students respond the most to upgrades to the bathrooms and playground areas. Once, I overheard some middle school students in Philadelphia say, "Principal EL must really like us—we now have automatic soap dispensers." I found this very amusing, as I loved them no less the day before the dispensers were installed. But these comments helped me understand how the students connected the improvement of the bathrooms to our love for them. Recently, I had new games painted on our schoolyard blacktop: four square, hopscotch, the round circle game, and others. I also refreshed the lines on our outdoor basketball court. Now, whenever buses are late picking kids up after school (which, given our bus driver shortage, can be often), they flock to the games in the schoolyard rather than waiting in the cafeteria, focused on their phones.

Strategy 2: Listen to and learn from students when they talk about their communities, their families, and their interests and goals.

Given the increasing diversity of our classrooms, listening to student's stories about their homes and communities is an excellent way for educators to expand their cultural competence, which can help to unlock some answers about student behavior, motivation, and attitudes. It also helps to cultivate the kinds of positive and consistent relationships that may help buffer the effects of any adversity students face. But before all this, listening to students when they share about themselves simply demonstrates that you care. Asking follow-up questions about students' interests, goals, and experiences—academic and personal—demonstrates to them that you are thinking of them as people and are invested in their emotional well-being.

Given how packed every school day already is, where can educators find time for these kinds of interactions and what could they focus on? Here are some ideas:

- **"Transportation talk" before and after school.** Have conversations about how students arrive at school and get back home each day if they are new to the school community (or if you are).

- **"Interest talk" as icebreakers, bell-ringer activities, or between classes.** Ask students what interests them inside and outside school. Especially early in the school year, it can be helpful to maintain a well-secured notebook or document full of details like this. As the school year continues, you will be able to draw on the important information in the notebook to highlight and celebrate notable moments for the students. You will also be able to identify opportunities to attend events away from school and learn even more about the students.

- **Regularly scheduled chats about anything.** Meet with students and their families regularly and maintain open lines of communication. These conversations with parents don't always have to be based on the student's behavior or academic performance. They should also focus on the emotional well-being of the students and their families. Think about starting your conversations with questions about family events (family reunions, family trips, birthdays), neighborhood events, sports- or arts-based activities outside school, and the health of other loved ones.

Strategy 3: Welcome all students with joy.

When adults with welcoming eyes and smiling faces are the first thing students see when they walk into school in the morning, we show them that we are people who have their best interests at heart and want to help them find joy in school and be successful. We become special to them when they can see they are special to us.

Here are some additional ways to make this clear:

- **State your intentions.** At the beginning of the school year, make sure students know you are happy to see them and glad they are in your classroom. These greetings should include words of affirmation and encouragement, along with positive statements like, "I look forward to getting to know you" and "Let's have a great year." Of course, learn all students' names as quickly as you can and be sure you are using the correct pronunciation.

- **Be happy to see them.** Greet students at the classroom door each day and applaud or recognize their presence or entrance. I have seen on social media that some teachers even go as far as to create individualized greetings or handshakes for each student. I love this. When students are dismissed each day, let them know you are excited to be their teacher and look forward to seeing them tomorrow.

- **Acknowledge them, always.** If you pass one of your students in the hallway, see them in the lunchroom or while on bus duty, or encounter them after school or on the weekend, acknowledge them with a warm smile, fist bump, or another greeting that's meaningful to you both. Tell them that you can't wait to see them in class.

Strategy 4: Share your own stories.

How did you decide to become a teacher? What kind of student were you? What's the *why* behind you showing up to teach them every day? Sharing stories about ourselves—both positive and uplifting ones and thought-provoking ones about struggle and lessons learned—reminds our students that we are human too and helps establish connections. This tactic can be a powerful one when you're trying to get everyone to participate in a classroom culture of love, inclusion, belonging, and support.

There are all kinds of ways to build on this strategy. Here are three easy ideas:

- **Encourage students to share stories about you with their families.** The connection-building can go both ways!
- **Expand your story audience to students' families.** They should be part of the community you build, so it can be helpful to include some brief information about your background or your *why* story in the letter you send home to families at the start of the year.
- **Include your personal "current events" in your communications with families**. Be brief but be real. And be sure to share how happy you are to be their child's teacher and how happy you are that they are part of your school community!

Being Crazy About Kids: How Students Benefit

When you are crazy about your kids and they know it, they will feel more comfortable in the classroom, more personally affirmed, and more excited about the learning you'll do together. They will feel a sense of ownership over the classroom and a sense of belonging. They will feel valued, safe, and less anxious. Linda Darling-Hammond once said, "The way the brain functions and grows, it needs safety, it needs warmth" (Riley & Terada, 2019 para. 8).

See students as important, treat them as important, and remind them how much they matter and that you are their champion and advocate. Good schools, great schools, and the people in them make students feel safe and loved. Adults believing in their students will help them reach their full potential.

The Second C: *Curious About Students' Lives Outside School*

Originally, I wanted the second of my Four Cs to be the word *caring*. But as I spoke with many teachers and administrators around the country, they expressed how easy it is for adults to *pretend* they care about kids. They pushed me to go deeper and think about a word that would capture the ideas I associate with truly caring about students: wanting to know about them, investing in them, and developing authentic connections. The word I settled on was *curiosity*. All learning beings with curiosity.

Curiosity is the fuel that powers everything in education. Relationships and connections are inspired and sustained by our willingness to learn as much about our students as possible. I believe an educator's impact is determined not solely by pedagogical practices they adopt but by their ability to be curious, learn, and apply that learning; this empowers them to adapt already strong pedagogy, as appropriate, for maximum effectiveness. As continuous learners, they can commit to creating classroom environments that thrive, providing instruction that's personalized, and facilitating the best outcomes for students. Lifelong learning includes taking a genuine interest in our students and their lives outside school. Students need to feel and hear that we want to know about them as people.

When the COVID-19 pandemic hit and our school went fully virtual, I worked hard to ensure every student had a laptop they could use at home. Those who needed home internet access received even more assistance. The key to getting a functional device into the hands and homes of every student was me learning to communicate more effectively and frequently with my staff, who were able to tell me where we could reach the students we'd lost track of during the early weeks of the pandemic. They even knew where students who had been transient were living. Thanks to these teachers' curiosity about their students, their hard work, and the relationships they had built with our students and families, we were able to serve so many more students in a powerful way during those difficult times.

When we are curious about their lives outside school, finding out if students have quiet places to study and read at home becomes important to us. The neighborhood they live in, their responsibilities at home, their resources and support, and who cares for them all inform our ability to meet their needs where *they* are and not just where we are. So, we must go to where they are and take them to where they should go academically, socially, and emotionally.

This also means that some of us will need to expand our understanding and acceptance of a changing society. No one is asking teachers to totally change their belief systems—not unless what they believe is that success is for some but not all, or that background, race, gender, and socioeconomic status determines the worth of a person. Any adult who believes this needs an immediate intervention or is simply in the wrong line of work.

Here are some strategic ways to foster and express curiosity about students' lives outside school.

Strategy 1: Check your personal biases.

Students come from all kinds of disparate living situations, including ones that will be different from yours and ones that you may have unexamined ideas about. It's imperative to be aware of your own biases, which are normal to have, and it's just as imperative, once you're aware of your biases, to work on moving beyond them. Here are some ideas that can help:

- **Get up to speed.** Form a support network with families and learn as much as you can about the cultural backgrounds of your students and how that might inform their behavior and attitudes. Invest in professional or personal development aimed at helping you better understand your beliefs and biases as well as how bias affects those who experience it as discrimination.
- **Stay mindful.** Be aware of how words, facial expressions, and body language can communicate rejection, prejudice, or bigotry. First impressions, especially if they are negative, are hard to change.
- **Engage in regular self-reflection.** Deep reflection allows us to think about and learn from our own experiences, and to avoid both conscious and unconscious biases.

Strategy 2: Show up for after-school or weekend events and competitions.

While teachers certainly have lives outside school with their own families and friends and outside commitments to attend to, showing up for student events will go a long way toward demonstrating that you are curious about your students as people.

Here are a few ways to approach the logistics:

- **First, do your research.** Discuss with students some of their outside activities (take notes!) so that the school can plan methods of support and participation.
- **Think: *strategic coverage.*** Staff members won't be able to attend every event or even as many as they might like to. I tell my staff that our school is a big family, so when even one adult goes, they represent all of us.
- **Use reports and recaps, if necessary.** If attending events is not possible, have students bring pictures, certificates, or trophies from events and games for "show-and-tell." This will also make a difference.

Strategy 3: Learn about and get involved in students' communities.

A teacher I met during my travels shared with me that children in her town rarely played in a neighborhood playground that was close to both the school and a low-income housing project. She didn't know if it was the students' love of video games that kept them inside or that the playground didn't feel safe to them; she just knew that when she drove by the playground, it was usually empty. When the teacher mentioned to her students that they never used the playground, a few replied that they had never seen *her* there either!

Now, I don't think those kids understood their teacher didn't live in the neighborhood, but they were speaking the truth. The teacher recognized this and responded by starting to take her own children to that neighborhood playground each weekend. Slowly but surely, children from the housing development started coming out to join them. A few more would come each weekend, and some days, they would have a large group. Not only was this a great way for the teacher to increase her connection with students, but it also led to some fascinating and fun conversations in class during the week. This small sacrifice of time and comfort also planted a seed for community interaction, which can certainly strengthen the home-school connection.

Here are some more ideas for venturing into and learning about your students' communities:

- **Research and leverage your resources.** Find intentional and specific ways to use the resources the community can provide: human (e.g., professionals, experts), institutional (e.g., local businesses, civic organizations, and government), natural (e.g., parks, forests, rivers), and cultural (e.g., creative and performing arts organizations).
- **Take educator field trips to local businesses.** Plan with a few colleagues to visit the local laundromat or community market to see students and learn more about what they do outside school hours.
- **Take educator field trips to local basketball courts and gyms (or wherever lots of kids spend their leisure time).** I found it so illuminating to see how many students who are very quiet and reserved in class get excited on the basketball courts. I mean, I heard some real trash talking! I even joined in a few games myself, and this led to a Friday evening and Saturday afternoon basketball program at school, where students and community volunteers got to interact in a positive and joyful environment.
- **Invite experts to school to speak to students about community events and opportunities.** Reach out to local arts organizations and to your parks and recreation department. I once invited the U.S. Forest Service Wildfire Prevention Campaign mascot "Smokey the Bear" to visit the students. One student was afraid to speak to Smokey but claimed he was only afraid because he was allergic to bears! Just another reason I'm crazy about kids!

Strategy 4: Create time to spend with students *in* school but *outside* the classroom.

There is a lot you can learn about students just by regularly sitting down with them at the lunch table! Outside the context of lessons, and if you avoid making stressful subjects like weekly or state assessments the topic of conversation, students can relax and enjoy their lunches while relating to their classmates and sharing a bit of their non-student selves with you. Those who may not have had the chance to establish or cultivate many friendships may even see positive social relationships modeled and developed.

Here are some more ideas for spending time with students outside the classroom but inside the school context:

- **Establish and lead book club discussions.** Let students members choose the books.
- **Join students in gym or recess to exercise or play sports with them.** Stretch first. Trust me on this.
- **Be a school trip chaperone.** Make sure the students who are new to the school or don't have many friends are in *your* group.
- **Attend after-school sporting events and other after-school activities.** Be open about it. You want to be seen! Step in after the event to congratulate the participants on their hard work, and if they're celebrating, mirror their enthusiasm.
- **If you're an administrator, think about covering classes for your teachers or co-teaching a lesson or two.** Teachers, you may not know this, but lots of administrators really miss teaching!

Being Curious About Their Lives: How Students Benefit

It is no secret that good teachers—*great* teachers—can change students' lives forever! Over my career, I have heard thousands of stories from current and former students about the relationships they developed with their teachers and how these have affected them. The success of many of these students and the connections they maintain are a huge testament to the power and benefit of strong adult-child relationships. Being curious about students' lives outside school demonstrates that we are interested in more than their grades and test scores. If we want to become great teachers and educators, we must first make connections with our students as people and be willing to meet them on multiple levels.

The best teachers and administrators are focused on the emotional well-being of their students. They are always trying to strengthen relationships with them and care as much about what they do outside school as we do about what they do inside our classrooms and our school. One reason is that we know what happens before and after the school day will have a serious impact—sometimes positive, sometimes negative—on what happens during it. Insight into these matters can lead to better instructional decisions and more effective approaches to behavior challenges, communication, and so on.

The Third C: *Consistent Adults in Students' Lives*

Supportive and consistent relationships are the foundation of a happy and successful life in school, at home, and in the community. Children with strong relationships with caring adults are more likely to be engaged at school and more motivated to succeed academically (Gruenert & Whitaker, 2024). Unfortunately, many children lack the stability and support of an adult who is there for them consistently over the days, weeks, and years.

I know firsthand because, when I was an adolescent, my father never visited my middle or high school—not even once. He never attended any of my basketball or baseball games, and there were hundreds of them. You might say that he was consistently absent from my life. This really had a negative impact on me. But I was blessed to have a very supportive, loving, and caring mother, who, along with my coaches, male mentors, and teachers, acted as my "village." It was their passionate and regular presence that helped me make it out of a very tough community.

When there are consistent adults in the lives of students, they can establish caring and meaningful relationships that help them thrive in challenging environments, communities, and situations. When we show students we care, have high expectations, and provide support to help them reach those expectations, we help them become resilient. We help them learn to embrace their struggles and failures.

Just as stability and reliability are important, instability can have a negative effect on adolescents. The research is just as strong: kids who live in stable households—where they know what to expect and feel and have security, health, and safety—do much better academically and emotionally (Sutherland, 2014). Transitions in family structure, housing, and food insecurity can threaten a child's sense of security. This is common knowledge, but it has also been backed by research. According to the Urban Institute (Sandstrom & Huerta, 2013), by the time children finish elementary school, more than one-third of them will experience their parents getting married, separated, or divorced. These transitions can be stressful for some children, but many transitions for children and their families can be positive as well. For example, a parent earning a promotion at work or getting a new job with a higher income can lead a new home and a safer community for the family and child but, at the same time, generate disruptions like moving away from neighborhood friends or cherished spaces. The key is having consistent adults in students' lives to provide the structure and stability that can steady them in times of disruption.

Children learn to become resilient and confident from their challenges and struggles, modeled and supported by trustworthy adults who can support them as they develop.

Here are some suggested ways to step up as consistent adults in students' lives.

Strategy 1: Set clear boundaries, expectations, and routines—and stick with them as long as they're effective.

Most teachers and administrators know that when boundaries and expectations are set, they provide children with a sense of safety and security. The children may not agree with all the rules, but they clearly understand what is expected. Consistent adults in school offer students the protection and structure they need to feel secure when away from home or when things at home, at school, or in the community change in ways big and small.

Here are some recommended ways to do this:

- **Establish routines for the start and end of class.** They can be especially helpful for new teachers or those who struggle with classroom management.
- **Prioritize consistency.** Provide students with (or collaborate with them to decide upon) consistent routines, procedures, and expectations for learning activities like note taking, retrieving supplies, carrying out lab activities, and studying, and give them clear, easily located instructions on how to carry these out.
- **Follow through with promises and consequences, as this is essential to establish trust.** I advise against giving second and third chances too many times. Oftentimes, students learn important lessons when we provide constructive consequences. Reading

to younger students in other grades and even helping the maintenance team clean, fix, and repair areas in the building are two great character-enhancing consequences. I have had students who had their own discipline issues over the years come to me and say, "I was reading to students earlier today and they were misbehaving. I hope I wasn't as bad as they are when I was young."

Strategy 2: Perfect routines throughout the year.

As mentioned earlier, trust is a key benefit of cultivating cultures that provide consistency and safety for all students, including those in the critical middle years' population. The qualification is being steady and reliable. We, as educators, often get it right early in the school year with lesson plans, structures, and routines. But sometimes, our work needs revision. As the year progresses, we can lose enthusiasm, leading to us becoming inconsistent and unpredictable in their implementation. And sometimes, routines that are effective in September are less so in February.

Here's what I recommend:

- **Monitor the effectiveness of your routines.** Focus on making sure procedures and schedules are reliable throughout the year. You might run some experiments, gather data, and get the students involved.
- **Make changes if you need to!** Consistency is a support for effectiveness, not a substitute for it! Be sure to support students as they deal with any changes.
- **Set the bar high, then higher.** As the year progresses, keep raising expectations for class routines and transitions, and keep students prepared throughout planning and engagement.

Strategy 3: Model and reinforce positive behavior and language.

A structured and organized classroom is a great place to set a positive example of the kinds of behavior, attitudes, and language you want students to adopt themselves.

One kind of modeling I particularly like to see is the power of positive thinking, communicated via classroom mantras, such as *I can be successful, I am kind to others,* and *I will respect my teachers and my school.* I was in a kindergarten classroom recently and was amazed by how well the young students memorized the class mantra. They stood up and recited it in unison. In doing this, they were also internalizing expectations.

Here are some other kinds of positive modeling and reinforcement I recommend:

- **Reinforce positive choices and actions.** It's fine to provide tangible rewards, at first, if this seems productive. As time goes on and your relationship with students deepens, snacks and prizes can wholly or mostly be replaced with verbal recognition and shout-outs from you, other students, other teachers, and school leaders.

- **Model emotional regulation.** When things get stressful or students are disruptive, one of the most valuable things you can do is keep your cool. Negative behaviors don't need to be rewarded with equally disruptive negative attention! But you can talk about frustration, about how it feels to get emotional in response to various kinds of triggers, and what to do to avoid getting swept up in them. Allowing students to see their teachers are human, can admit mistakes, and can work to be better has great value.

- **Model how to speak respectfully and appropriately in various circumstances.** Teaching students to be aware of their surroundings and audience when they speak and to focus on what they are saying and how they are saying it will benefit them tremendously when they are in college and starting their careers. Code switching— with spoken language *and* body language—is an important form of communication. Minority students especially often have to master code switching in different environments as a defense mechanism against biases and misconceptions.

- **Model kindness and empathy.** There have been many times when a student came to me disruptive and upset and I simply told the student, "I loved you before I ever met you, and there isn't anything you can do to change that." When I see students who are not happy in school, I look for ways to be more inclusive and enhance their sense of belonging by inviting them to join other students and me at lunch or after school to talk. These methods allowed me to diffuse or deescalate many potential problems.

Strategy 4: Be an ongoing, joyful influence in the lives of students.

For young people, consistent adults provide stability, a sense of trust, and valuable connections. But those same students also need adults who care about them, value their input and opinions, and bring happiness to school with them each day. Don't get me wrong: every day won't be like Disney World! I have had some rough days at school, trust me. But even on the hard days, I tried to be a positive influence on my students by showing up and pushing through my challenges, being a good role model and example, and finding joyful ways to make their day better. Here are some ways to be a consistent and joyful influence:

- **Take an interest in students' lives and show them that you care.** This means helping them to discover their passion and talking to them about other careers you considered (or even had) before you decided to be an educator that might appeal to them. It means introducing students to role models in the community. It means respecting their perspectives and recognizing their achievements. It means providing guidance, academic scaffolds, and even social support. Consider starting a Gentlemen's or Gentleladies' Club where students can learn formal table manners, how to shake hands at an interview or when meeting someone for the first time, and even how to dress for business or formal events. All of these are great skills that they will use in the future.
- **Be a good role model.** Let students see you show grace and empathy in class. We ask young people all the time to be forgiving and understanding. We must practice what we preach. We can be such positive influences and examples for students when we instill values like respect and integrity but also model them as well. Introduce creative and engaging lessons using the skills and techniques learned in professional development sessions, and let students know you implemented these lessons after learning them in your

own classes. This shows them the value of learning in their classes and how you are still a learner as the teacher. Improving your teaching continuously will be the key to engaging students and keeping them joyful and hungry to learn in the classroom.

- **Become a part of students' "village" and let them know you embrace that role.** A great way to do this is to check on them and give students a chance to speak their mind on those hard days. Some of them struggle at home and in the community and value having someone they can talk to about their issues. When you take an authentic interest in students' lives, and not just on the good days, they will begin to enjoy being in your class each day. They may not always show it, but students genuinely value adult respect and attention. I often used my own life as an example for students and shared with them that I had some struggles of my own—and still do. I always remember to tell them about teachers I had who were a part of my village and showed care and concern for me. I stress that they taught me that there was nothing wrong with me and it was OK to make mistakes and then try again.

- **Focus on students' emotional needs.** Developing good and healthy relationships and friendships is so important. Assist them with improving their patience and emotional regulation. Encourage them to have a growth mindset and inspire them to overcome the battles they face. We can't prevent adversity, but we can help students to see it differently and understand that they are not fighting those battles alone. Let them know they are supported and surrounded by teachers and other adults who are trustworthy and have character and lots of love in their hearts.

Being a Consistent Adult in Their Lives: How Students Benefit

The benefits of consistent adults and structures in students' lives are numerous. When young people have safety and predictability in their learning environment and at home, trusting adults and building relationships with school staff and their families become easier. Consistent encouragement, praise, and acknowledgment matter. Having positive relationships at school does not just mean that children are taught academics and treated kindly by adults. It also means that schools foster and support students' emotional well-being through those relationships. When children feel safe in the consistent relationships they develop in school, they become more confident and independent, and better prepared to face life's challenges. These relationships are important to students becoming resilient and learning to overcome obstacles. When there are strong relationships between students and adults in school and in the community, all members of that community can thrive.

The Fourth C: *A Culture of Love, Support, and High Expectations*

A positive school culture in which children and adults feel loved and supported is what every teacher, administrator, and parent hope for.

Teachers are more likely to stay in the profession when legislators and policymakers fund our schools and programs appropriately, and school systems commit to cultivate thriving and inclusive school cultures. When we create joyful and supportive school cultures for our students and teachers, they stay. District and school leaders have known for decades that developing cultures of love, joy, and high expectations is key to safe and successful schools.

Understanding the importance of positive school cultures has not been the challenge over the years. The problem is more complex. Many principals, including myself, often struggle to clearly define, describe, and sustain a positive school culture. We often think the culture is good when teachers smile and students succeed, and it's not good when a few teachers resign or rates of discipline increase. Yet a positive school culture is about so much more. It's grounded in its core beliefs and behaviors. In a strong school culture, the positive messages teachers and staff receive daily impact their interactions with colleagues and students. These messages communicate authenticity, honesty, and collaboration. They are sent by administrators and others in the school and can be intentional and unintentional.

Teachers and staff appreciate working in school cultures where each person in the school community has an essential role (Kafele, 2019). Diversity, equity, and inclusion efforts can positively affect school culture and help more members of the school community feel they have a stake and significance. All school community members need to feel that their ideas and concerns are being heard, respected, and valued.

When the principal or school leader listens to others and spends time and energy on understanding all community members, the entire school, including staff, students, and parents, begins to feel like they understand their roles. Listening can be healing, especially for members of underserved and marginalized communities.

The past few years have been challenging and have affected school cultures everywhere. Teachers, students, and families are not in a good place socially or emotionally, and we need to help them get better. As principals and administrators, we need to think differently about the emotional well-being of our staff and students. For years, they have dealt with underfunded schools, overcrowded classrooms, and increased school violence. Schools that neglect to focus on cultivating school cultures that create love and joy for students and teachers will struggle to meet many of their needs in the coming years. Teacher appreciation must happen beyond the month of May. Pep rallies and assemblies should occur on a regular basis. We can't go back to the status quo when creating cultures of positivity and joy for our students and staff. Celebrating the hard work, progress and success of our staff and students must be the norm—not a once- or twice-a-year thing.

Here are some strategies for creating this kind of culture. You'll find lots more detail in the pages ahead.

Strategy 1: Be visible and engaged.

Spending time with students and staff and showing care and concern for them in their spaces is a compelling way for a leader to model empathy and understanding. What does this mean?

- **Prioritize student care.** Focus on building and sustaining strong adult-child relationships, establishing effective communication around student support, and encouraging positive conversations on teaching and learning.
- **Provide forums for positive interaction.** Foster a culture of collaboration between all members of the school community by

hosting informal meetings with teachers, Back to School Night events, Literacy and Math Nights at school, and open houses for parents and community members.

Strategy 2: Be adaptive and open to change.

School cultures do not change in a day, week, or month and take years to shift and change. Real, sustainable change requires leaders to reflect and grow both personally and professionally (Gruenert & Whitaker, 2024). That growth comes from attending leadership conferences, connecting with other leaders, reading great books on leadership, and finding mentors. We must become learners and listeners, and comfortable with being vulnerable. There will be times when we need to empower and uplift others, and there will also be times when we should lend an empathetic ear.

Here are some ways to model adaptive leadership:

- **Keep learning.** Regularly attend professional development meetings with teachers as well as sessions focused on unpacking the curriculum.
- **Focus on positive communication.** Celebrating and including all members of the school community helps to keep everyone feeling safe and supported during challenging times. Define and use those messages in classrooms, halls, newsletters that go home, social media, and on the school website. Monitor the exchanges and be prepared to adjust or redirect messaging in light of feedback.
- **Work on expanding your emotional intelligence.** An adaptive leader seeks to create a caring and loving school culture based on the beliefs, hopes, dreams, and talents of their staff. Cultivating strong relationships requires much work and commitment. Sustaining a positive and uplifting culture is even more challenging because the school community must continue to move in the same direction, commit to its goals, and communicate positive messages daily. The adaptive leader needs a strong sense of emotional intelligence to succeed.

Strategy 3: Keep communication lines open and listen to all stakeholders.

School culture is much stronger when communication about school culture, norms, challenges, and triumphs is ongoing and honest, and when stakeholders inside and outside the school feel they are a valuable part of an ongoing conversation. Effective communication that prioritizes listening to stakeholders helps ensure that no member in the school community feels isolated or excluded. It sends the message that leadership wants to establish strong relationships and deep connections with stakeholders because their contributions are powerful and necessary.

Here are some ideas for boosting the quality and frequency of communication and ensuring stakeholders feel valued as part of an inclusive school community:

- **Provide a regular way for the community to hear directly from the principal or other administrators.** Effective and consistent communication is the lifeline of the school that engages families and community members. Using positive messages early in the school year helps to build rapport and connections with stakeholders.

- **Get to know stakeholders and understand their perspectives on how the school can impact the community.** Doing so will improve the input and responses you receive from them. When we listen as leaders and educators, we validate their perspectives. Listen intently in meetings and conferences and gather input from the school community to improve the culture of the school.

- **Recognize and celebrate community stakeholders.** This is a way to both strengthen relationships and introduce students to local heroes. Over the years at my school, we have hosted "Leadership Days" where local community members come to the school for a morning or afternoon visit and a tour with students. They then spend time listening to student speeches on leadership, poetry, and book readings. Community members share their leadership journeys. I think of this as local curriculum.

Strategy 4: Set high expectations and believe that all children can be successful.

Love is a strong word and a strong emotion, and it should be felt in every area of the school! Adding love and support to the foundation of your school culture, along with high expectations for all students and families, will allow teachers and students to be engaged and work together. Develop a mindset in your school that *effort* will support student success more than intrinsic factors or student background (Tomlinson, 2014).

Here is how you might go about it:

- **Communicate, demonstrate, and cultivate expectations and beliefs early and often.** Students thrive in a safe and engaging classroom environment with clear expectations.
- **Learn how to set expectations that are both high and appropriate.** Data is your ally here. Gather information about your students' gifts and challenges, their academic histories, and their preferred learning styles. Read up on the concept and practice of "teaching up" (Tomlinson, 2023).
- **Focus on balancing rigor and joy.** When expectations are high and the support is present, teachers become "warm demanders," educators who build strong relationships and hold students to high standards (Hammond, 2014). This feeling of high expectations for students and adults permeates throughout the school, and students and parents can feel that we are meeting the diverse needs of our school family.

When we help students become their best selves, continually raise the bar, and motivate them to reach that bar, we instill confidence and agency. When we create a culture of belief as school leaders and educators, and have high expectations of *ourselves*, too, we communicate a message to the entire school and the outside community that all of us share in the responsibility for the success of our children. That's why I started my chess program. I wanted to show the school, community, and world that a challenging game like chess was not only something students could play but also something they could master.

A Culture of Caring, Positivity, and High Expectations: How Students Benefit

Creating and cultivating cultures of caring, positivity, and high expectations fosters a sense of ownership within the school community—the idea that that this building, these colleagues and children, and this mission are *ours* and worth fighting for. It powers ongoing cooperation—often creative and innovative—to figure out and pursue what is best for kids. Trust, psychological safety, and resilience become the norm when students feel seen and heard.

Reflect & Take Action

Educators—teachers, administrators, district leaders—have the power to strengthen the structures and practices that foster curiosity, trust, consistency, school culture, and positive relationships. I want to inspire educators to think differently about how we show up for kids and collaborate with our colleagues to improve our profession and schools. If we genuinely want to give every student what they need to be successful in these challenging times, it will be necessary for us to develop cultures of trust, love, and support in every school.

As we advocate for this equity, we can also enhance our current school cultures and resources by building healthy relationships among adults and students. Those relationships have the power to shape a child's future and increase their engagement in school and in the community. We can increase the strength of our support by being crazy about our kids, curious about their lives inside and outside school, consistent in our efforts to support and be present for our students, and loving in our passion for developing school cultures that promote deep connections and support.

Reflection questions

Take a moment to reflect on Chapter 1 and how it applies to your unique district, school, classroom, and students. Consider:

1. Which of the Four Cs do your students need most right now? Why?
2. How can you embrace the Four Cs in your career and life this week? This month? This year?

Next steps

True change requires action. Empower the bigger picture by working on long-term goals:

- Include the Four Cs in your yearly and semester planning, identifying the strategies you will use to prioritize them.
- Choose one of the Cs and create a plan for how you'll incorporate its associated strategies into your daily work. At the end of each semester, take time to reflect on and refine your plan.
- Pair with a close colleague or team member who is also focusing on the same C to extend and refine your efforts collaboratively. Share your focus and plan refinements with a mentor for accountability.

2

Trauma-Informed Practice

In my early days as a middle school principal in Wilmington, Delaware, I had a student who was very smart, athletic, and spoke his mind often but sometimes struggled with his behavior. At home, he had a strong single mom who was his rock and his foundation. He also had some amazing siblings and friends. Growing up in Wilmington, a place with one of the highest per capita murder rates in the country, you needed a tight circle around you.

Nah'Shon Hyland, or "Bones," as his friends referred to him, was not only a good basketball player; he was also a promising chess player. (I wanted him to focus more on chess, but he just loved basketball, and that was fine!) When Bones completed 8th grade with us, he went on to St. Georges Technical High School in Middletown, Delaware, and became a stand-out basketball player. Not just good, but *really* good: named to the All-State team over multiple years and capturing the attention of many college basketball programs.

One evening in March 2018, when Bones was 17, all that he had worked for came crashing down on him. He was home with his grandmother and baby cousins when the Wilmington Fire Department responded to a house fire at their home. Bones had to jump from a second-floor bedroom window to save his life and suffered a serious knee injury when he landed on the ground. His grandmother and one cousin didn't survive. The loss was devastating. In addition, doctors told Bones that basketball was probably over for him. He had a torn patella tendon, and even after surgery, he would have his work cut out to play again, let alone compete at the level he had played before.

But for Bones, quitting was not an option. He worked hard at rehabilitation after surgery, often using our middle school gym to work himself back into shape. He was determined to play at the college level, and he proved all the doctors wrong. When he returned to play basketball during his senior year in high school, he scored 50 points in three consecutive games. Bones went on to star for Virginia Commonwealth University and was drafted by the Denver Nuggets in the first round of the 2021 NBA draft. In his rookie season, he scored 27 points against LeBron James and the Lakers, and he now plays for the Los Angeles Clippers.

Nah'Shon Hyland often returns to his old neighborhood and former schools to host basketball camps and community events, and to inspire the young people there. His story is one of overcoming trauma, and he embodies determination and resilience. I tell his story because there are students like Bones sitting in classrooms across the country, and they need trauma-informed teachers and leaders.

What Does *Trauma-Informed* Mean?

Human minds and bodies are equipped to survive. When chased by a dog on the street or a bear in the woods, we enter "fight or flight" mode to help us stay alert and alive. Our heart rate and blood pressure rise. Our perception of pain dulls. We tense up, full of adrenaline. Other physical and mental tasks get put on the back burner, as we focus all our energy on the most important task at hand: *survival* (Gagliardi, 2023).

While we may not face life-or-death, dog-or-bear situations each day, we do experience stressors that can send us into fight-or-flight mode. This state isn't triggered often in healthy environments where we feel safe, secure, and stable. But for many of our students, fight-or-flight stressors are the norm. From health issues and racial injustice to school shootings, poverty, bullying, and abuse, too many are nearly *living* in a state of fight-or-flight each day. They're in survival mode: continually on edge and under threat. This is trauma, the physical, mental, and emotional response a person feels when trying to cope with the memory and lasting effects of painful events.

Our students are dealing with trauma in and out of school. Many are *hypervigilant*, always on the lookout for the next threat. As a result, they can perceive small, everyday stressors—an assignment deadline, pop quiz, or school project—as a threat. The Centers for Disease Control and Prevention (Chatterjee, 2019) identify trauma as the greatest public health issue our children face in these times. Research tells us that at least two in three students have faced at least one traumatic event by the time they reach high school (American University School of Education, 2021). For educators who work in urban or rural areas, those numbers are even higher. Then think about the COVID-19 pandemic, which affected all children, but it affected each child *differently*; some were certainly left with trauma.

Trauma is a unique, individualized experience because it's based on perception, history, and resilience (Burke Harris, 2018). It can stem from, or be compounded by, anything from grief, neglect, and physical abuse or injury to illness, drug abuse, instability at home, loss of family members or friends, transience, homelessness, bullying, and social media. It affects students' ability to form healthy relationships, behave appropriately, manage emotions, and achieve academic goals. Students with a history of trauma have lower GPAs, higher dropout rates, and lower employment rates (American University School of Education, 2021).

Trauma-informed teaching and leadership is about refusing to ignore these difficult topics and diving in head-first to understand and address them (Kaufman, n.d.). It's built on five core principles:

1. **Relationship building.** Foster positive relationships with students and families to ensure they have anchors and support.
2. **Confidence building.** Give students opportunities to feel safe, strong, and secure in their environment so that they can feel more in control of their lives and destiny.
3. **Communication.** Work to understand students' backstories and challenges so you can provide the unique support they need.
4. **Modeling.** Set an example of constructive ways to regulate emotions, respond to stress, and manage conflict.
5. **Restorative discipline.** Keep cool and let students know conflict, mistakes, and stress are OK and things they can learn to navigate.

Advocate for fairness, and rather than punish negative behavior, help students transform it into something positive.

In short, a trauma-informed educational practice impacts students inside and outside the classroom by building relationships and increasing confidence and communication (see Figure 2.1).

FIGURE 2.1
The Core Principles of Trauma-Informed Practice

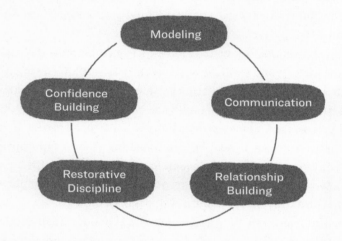

An Educator's Responsibility

It is difficult for teachers to educate hungry and tired students who struggle to focus. I know because I used to be one of those students. When I think back to my own childhood, I can recall many times that my 3rd and 4th grade teachers provided morning and afternoon snacks for me and the other hungry kids in my classroom. They used their own money to buy these snacks, as thousands of teachers do every day, because they knew how many kids came to school tired and hungry, and they knew how hunger and fatigue build as the school day goes on.

But for some reason, back at the start of my career, I did not give my students this kind of understanding and grace. I had somehow convinced myself that they just needed to be responsible and held accountable when they weren't. My perspective changed over time, and a catalyst was reading a poem called "'Cause I Ain't Got a Pencil" by Joshua T. Dickerson (2014), a teacher in Georgia. You can find the poem online. It is short and powerful, relaying how a student helps their younger sister get ready for school. Their parents aren't home, and they have no clean clothes or electricity. They make it to school early to get a good breakfast. When the older sibling finally sits down in class, the teacher fusses because the kid doesn't have a pencil.

Sadly, that teacher was me for a good part of my career! *I* was the one fussing over the pencils and supplies students lacked instead of thinking about the trauma and adversity they had to face and overcome each day. Just like in the poem, my students had to clean up early in the morning after late-night parties or stay up late to help give medication to parents or elderly grandparents. Finding a pencil was the least of their worries. They had to find their younger sisters or brothers, find a meal or clean clothes, or even find the strength just to make it to school each day.

Many of my students experienced some of the same adversity I did: poverty, lack of healthcare, food insecurity, and homelessness. How could I have forgotten how grateful I'd been for the amazing teachers who had looked after me, even though many of them didn't look *like* me or come from the same community? Some of the students I fussed at for forgetting school supplies were from my very own community. It was like looking in a mirror and not recognizing myself, maybe because what I saw reflected was such a distorted vision of what I wanted to see. I had to find my way back to my true passion for mentoring, connecting, and building relationships. Yes, I had to learn how to reach and connect with kids in a way that reflected my real values. It was necessary for their survival and for mine. It was time for a reset.

In the same way, we need our school systems to reset to better support students living with trauma and meet their needs. Again, I know this because I was one of those kids: no father around and living in public housing in an unstable, crime-riddled community. I am being very honest and open right now, early on in this book, because honesty and authenticity allow us to grow as educators, build trust, and foster empathy.

Sometimes, we have to peel back the layers of the external rules to get back to empathetic, inspirational teaching and leadership that empower others. *This* is what we need in our schools and nation right now.

No one should have to read the pencil poem as many times as I did. The first time I read it, I knew it was speaking to me. It reminded me of my childhood struggles. I had a trauma response. Yet, I kept going back to it, and each time I read it, I found myself thinking about a different student who had reported to school without a pencil, a textbook, lunch, or a stable home life. I thought about Rodney, Shawn, Dante, and so many others. I thought about Lovisha, one of the first young ladies to join our Saturday tutoring group. I thought about Kenyetta, who helped us establish our chess program on a national level. The first time I read the poem, I had an epiphany. But the frequent rereads confirmed that I needed to find a different path. Finding my purpose was clearly on my mind, but it was most of all in my heart! I felt the reality of the trials and tribulations our students weather each day. I keep it and other inspirational pieces near me to encourage and ignite my soul as an educator. I recommend you do the same if you can.

Daily reminders and reflections keep us fresh, joyful, and strong. We need constant prompting to become teachers who give students everything they need to succeed. Their success in school and life requires us to intentionally focus on issues of equity, social justice, trauma, mentoring, and culturally responsive teaching; this mentality will be necessary for all of us. Believe me: providing pencils and other supplies costs much less than paying to rehabilitate adults in our prison system or, sadly, paying for the funerals of the young people we lose.

As educators, we must constantly remind ourselves of the lives our students lead outside the classroom. We must never assume what goes on behind the scenes. When a student acts out, we must step back. Instead of reacting, punishing, and criticizing, we must seek to understand the root of the problem. We can't always look for what is wrong with the child, but we can try to find out what they believe may have caused the issue or trauma they are dealing with. To see the world from their perspective. This is the heart of being a trauma-informed teacher and leader: it's about being curious, not critical; understanding, not uncompromising; and accepting, not authoritarian.

Increasing Your Understanding

The path to becoming a trauma-informed teacher and leader is lit by the Four Cs. To understand trauma-informed theory and practices, we must be curious about the lives of students outside school and gain awareness of their experiences and the influences that impact their lives. To effectively apply trauma-informed practices, we must be consistent adults in these students' lives. When we foster a supportive classroom that promotes safety, consistency, and strong relationships, we build trust with our students that supports engagement in school, academic success, and emotional health. There are three sources you can turn to as you increase your understanding of trauma-informed theory and practices: self-directed learning, personal reflection, and your students themselves.

Self-directed learning

Read books and articles on trauma-informed teaching and leadership, focusing on social-emotional learning practices that empower empathy and compassion. Books that I recommend include *Fostering Resilient Learners* (Souers & Hall, 2016); *Building Trauma Sensitive Schools* (Alexander, 2019); *Trauma-Sensitive School Leadership* (Ziegler et al., 2022); *Trauma Responsive Pedagogy* (Casimir & Baker, 2024); *Relationship, Responsibility, and Regulation* (Souers & Hall, 2019); and *Every Connection Matters* (Creekmore & Creekmore, 2024).

Self-reflection and self-improvement

It's difficult to guide others on the path to healing when we're weighed down by our own wounds. Work on yourself. Uncover, unpack, and understand your own trauma. Invest in your own well-being. Learn to regulate your own emotions and take accountability for your own behavior. Through reflection and reconciliation, you can come to better distinguish your personal trauma from your students', which is conducive to creating a space of joy, healing, and safety for everyone.

Here are some questions to ask yourself:

- What trauma have I faced in my life? How did I recognize it as trauma?

- Have I fully overcome the trauma I faced? If so, how? If not, what progress have I made, and how did I do that?
- Who were the people who helped to facilitate my healing and growth? How did they help me?
- What resources am I employing that are necessary for the healing and growth of my students?

Your students themselves

Trauma-informed teaching puts relationships before assignments, lectures, and tests. If these relationships fail to form—if the trauma is never addressed—your students will find it hard to be mentally, emotionally, or socially present. Trauma can function as a block that keeps students from listening and learning. So get to know who your students are. Spend time in their communities. Do your best to understand the trauma they're going through, how it affects them, and how you can help (Venet, 2021).

Strategies for Trauma-Informed Practice

When it comes to more specific ways to implement trauma-informed teaching and leadership, I can recommend several strategies.

Strategy 1: Recognize that students are individuals with varying experiences that affect their learning.

Trauma-informed teaching requires us to respect and support our students' differences—and to overcome any personal biases, assumptions, and beliefs that get in the way of serving all students with care and respect. To form meaningful, individual relationships, we must understand what makes our students *individuals*!

Here are some ways to implement this strategy:

- **Set aside dedicated time to listen to and learn from students.** Maybe this is lunch with students in the classroom, the cafeteria, your office, or the schoolyard. Maybe it's "office hours" or listening to kids during bus dismissal or an after-school program. Their stories and experiences are so rich and enlightening. Listening to their goals, hopes, and dreams can promote a sense of collaboration and connection. Something as simple as always greeting students at the door or writing them positive messages can make a tremendous impact on their self-esteem and sense of belonging.

- **Attend outside events and activities in the community.** When the students see you in the community or at outside activities, their eyes light up with excitement as if they have not seen you in months. They love feeling like their world beyond school matters to their teachers and administrators. You don't have to attend sporting events; students enjoy seeing us at dance recitals, in church, or at their birthday parties. They just want to know that we are curious about the lives they lead. I would recommend that when you attend games or other sports and activities, you do not attend alone. Take another staff member with you or a family member who is comfortable spending time with community members in support of your efforts to make these authentic connections.

- **Research and notice.** Find out where students are coming to school from and where they are going after. Find out both *from whom* they come and *to whom* they go. It is important to understand their household makeup. Are they being raised by a mother or grandmother? Do they have Dad at home or in their lives? What positive male or female role models are they connected with in the community? This information fills in the gaps and can inform positive action. Learning if our students live in an apartment, a home, housing projects, a shelter, or a foster home helps us to serve them better.

- **Work with other members of the school community.** School counselors and social workers can provide valuable insight about students' lives outside school as well as guidance on how to respond, if their professional judgment indicates a response is needed. They can, for example, inform teachers if a student might benefit from meals over the weekend. Parent and community coordinators are another great asset when trying to find ways to support students and their families with housing and utilities, which might include connecting with local faith-based organizations or churches to source clothing and other resources.

This is where curiosity about our students becomes vital. It's not that we want to "pry," but because we are committed to learning how best to support every single student in our orbit.

Strategy 2: Adopt a "holistic school" mindset.

Everyone involved in your school should be actively trained and involved in the effort to become trauma-informed. It's not just a one-time practice but a holistic perspective, mindset, and lens to approaching student learning (Robertson et al., 2018). Leadership must revisit and reimagine their school's overarching programs, initiatives, and models.

Here are some ways to implement this strategy:

- **Provide formal professional development training.** Set up trauma-informed seminars and training sessions, along with small-group accountability sessions, and ongoing conversations about diversity, equity, and inclusion. When schools foster inclusivity and adopt a comprehensive approach to trauma awareness, they can inspire students, staff, and parents to be curious about how trauma affects behavior and learning, ask questions, and embrace a sense of empathy and social responsibility. As teachers, staff, and administrators learn both the importance and application of trauma-informed practices, they can change how they reach students. This education should focus not just on the *what* but on the *how* as well. Teachers need actionable steps and plans to shift to a holistic trauma-informed mindset.
- **Implement trauma-informed teaching practices consistently in classrooms, hallways, and beyond.** Invest in authentic diversity, equity, and inclusion development. All students and staff members need to feel included, respected, valued, understood, and appreciated. Schools can also foster a culture where students and staff learn to appreciate diversity and differences and respect the opinions of others. This can be done through classroom debates and hosting forums.
- **Teach critical thinking, problem solving, creativity, and resilience.** These skills are vital to the success of students and adults in our changing world.

- **Research and launch a high-quality social-emotional learning (SEL) program.** These programs recognize the need for cultural competence, sensitivity, and responsiveness in relationships. They also help educators gain a better understanding of the principles and practice of both cultural competence and culturally responsive teaching. By supporting the development of self-awareness, emotional regulation, empathy, collaboration, and togetherness, they address the ultimate aim of quality education, which is developing the necessary social, emotional, and cognitive skills for lifelong success.

Strategy 3: Create a predictable, consistent, and secure learning environment.

Consistency and predictability are important for all students, but children impacted by trauma need them even more. Teachers and administrators must find ways to use best practices to create, maintain, and sustain positive school and classroom cultures that promote consistency and proper guidance (Minahan, 2019).

Traumatized students rely on consistency and predictability to feel safe and secure in school; however, we can neither expect nor demand that *they* be consistent and predictable in their behavior. Healing from and processing trauma is not a linear journey; there will be ups, downs, twists, and turns along the way. Plan for this. Plan for incredible progress *and* temporary setbacks, and model the responses to both that you want students to embrace. Be patient with them, demonstrate your patience through consistency, and be generous with the positive reinforcement.

Being consistent doesn't mean you shouldn't be adaptive; as we know, flexibility is necessary to meet our students where they are. In this profession, flexibility also helps to ensure longevity: we adjust and adapt our teaching to meet student needs, support their growth, and draw value from the work we do. But classroom consistency—things like standard study or test preparation routines, standard transition practices, clear and consistently enforced sets of expectations—is an anchor for students who might not know what environment they'll be going home to. Your classroom can be the one place they know they will be treated well, respected, and understood.

Here are some other ways to create a predictable and secure learning environment:

- **Accentuate the positive.** Focus less on "discipline and consequences" and more on physical and emotional safety, joy, and inclusion. This means rethinking punishment as an opportunity for healing and repair.
- **Worry less about what is wrong and more about what is needed—and what is possible.** Students affected by trauma need empathy and patience to heal and grow!
- **Redefine in-school suspension as a calm, safe haven.** Look for ways to use the time to nurture student stamina and teach students strategies for persistence, coping with frustration, and behavioral modification.

Strategy 4: Flip the script.

When children are stuck in a certain negative behavior, thought, or feeling, one of the best ways to free them from this trap is to help them "flip the script": change direction or shift their focus.

Here's what I mean: A traumatized student might have developed the habit of thinking a negative thought about themselves or others.

I'm never good enough.

I don't know how to do anything.

I always get in trouble.

Those teachers hate me. Those kids hate me.

When triggered or struggling, these students can easily get stuck in a negative thought cycle. Help them flip the script! In practical terms, this might mean shifting them onto a different, individual activity; asking them to take a break in a calm corner of the classroom set up with a beanbag chair or two; or playing a short game designed to support emotional regulation.

Now, the goal isn't to simply avoid all negative thoughts; however, rehashing the negative thought can feel like a punishment. Flip the script by focusing on reinforcing and rewarding their positive behavior.

There is so much power in acknowledgment. In my experience, acknowledging students' success and efforts motivates them to follow the rules and meet our expectations for behavior and academic outcomes. Acknowledging a young person, seeing them, hearing them, and making sure they know they and their efforts are important can combat some of the effects of trauma by fostering a sense of belonging, resilience, self-esteem, confidence, and empowerment. At the heart of it all, *that's* the mission of trauma-informed teaching: to help every single child feel included, accepted, and loved no matter what's happening outside the classroom. And look! We are back to being crazy about kids, curious about their lives, a consistent presence in their lives, and dedicating ourselves to creating a culture of love—a space for children to learn and heal and to chart their own paths forward, fueled by the assurance that their teachers and mentors know them, their culture, and their stories. There's great security in knowing that their entire school community supports them today and will support them tomorrow, next week, next semester, and beyond.

Reflect & Take Action

The hard truth is that some of our students live each day on a battlefield, and simply showing up to school is a victory. The proper response is to make our schools, classrooms, and districts calm, safe, respectful places. The relationships developed in school are an especially important factor in building resilience in trauma-affected students. They are building blocks for academic success and increased social emotional learning.

We must also acknowledge that inequity at school can be a source of trauma as well. It's imperative that educators learn about and employ trauma-informed practices. By seeking to understand what's going on inside and outside school, and then responding accordingly, we can make school a sanctuary of safety, learning, and possibility for students who are navigating trauma.

Reflection questions

Take a moment to reflect on Chapter 2 and how it applies to your unique district, school, classroom, and students. Consider:

1. Are you aware of any trauma your students may be experiencing? How could you increase your awareness and understanding of this trauma?
2. Can you identify any trauma you faced as a child or adult that informs how you teach or lead students who are dealing with trauma?
3. How might your classroom and school feel safe to your students? How might it feel unsafe?
4. How are you incorporating the five core principles of trauma-informed teaching (see p. 43) in your relationship-building efforts?
5. As a trauma-informed teacher and leader, how are you ensuring that students feel included, valued, and respected in school?

Next steps

True change requires action. Empower the bigger picture by working on long-term goals:

- Incorporate trauma-informed theories and strategies into your lesson plans and preparation each week, month, semester, and year.
- Schedule regular times to better get to know students, their families, and their stories.

3

Engaging, Challenging, and Joyful Classrooms

As I walked into a classroom with my visitors from our state department of education, I silently prayed that my students would not embarrass me. No, not because of their behavior or work habits, but because of their propensity to complain to *anyone* who would listen about how often I promise them pizza and how rarely I deliver! Like all principals, I know that if you want to get students to cooperate, the promise of a hot pizza will go a long way; but once those 3rd graders reach the 7th and 8th grades, they are wise to our old tricks. Of course, I have treated them to pizza quite a few times, but they never seem to remember those occasions!

Our school receives lots of support from the Delaware Department of Education. Part of that support involves school visits—not so much for evaluation or added pressure but to get a general sense of the school's culture and how the students and teachers are doing. On this particular day, they saw a lot of joy and a lot of learning. For example, our 8th grade English language arts (ELA) students were having a debate facilitated by their teacher, Candace Charles-Inniss. She has been an amazing teacher at our school for almost two decades, and the students enjoy attending her class. Don't get me wrong: Mrs. Inniss is no pushover! She sets high standards and is tough on her kids, but she shows them tons of love and does everything she can to keep them engaged and excited. On this day, the 8th graders were debating topics like student choice in school uniforms and whether college athletes should be paid. Who was acting as the judge in this debate? Our 7th grade students. Mrs. Inniss gave them an evaluation rubric to follow, and they were engaged and a part of the process. Next year, as 8th graders, *they* would be the debaters, and their participation here showed them very clearly what would be expected of them. Needless to say, our visitors from the state were impressed, and I was amazed all over again at how well this teacher could engage students in a challenging but joyful classroom.

This is what the Four Cs are truly about: generating joy and celebrating students in a supportive, learning-focused environment. I've seen it happen over and over again: when we make our classrooms interesting and engaging, and when we show up every day to share our own positive stories about our learning experiences, students get more excited about managing their own learning and participating in a culture of love, respect, and hope. During this debate, our students were happy and engaged. They were making choices and rising to challenges. They were collaborating in ways that expanded everyone's understanding. That's a learning community.

There is so much to gain when educators cultivate strong relationships and connections with students and families. We can't prevent the adversity they will face or the obstacles in their lives, but we can help them view challenges differently and become more resilient in the process.

The Qualities and Value of Engaging, Challenging, and Joyful Classrooms

As educators, we do what we do to positively affect the lives of our students. We want to guide them, shape their minds, and equip them with the skills and tools for understanding they need to be well-balanced, contributing members of society. But many obstacles stand in the way of our students finding success, joy, and learning in schools, including funding issues, political battles, teacher shortages, school and community violence, the banning of books, behavioral problems, lack of parental support, and negative bias related to their socioeconomic status, perceived intellectual ability, or race. Gorski (2018) reminds us that few of the struggles and barriers students face have any inherent basis in intellectual ability or race. As teachers and administrators, we need a full sense of what we're up against; sometimes, as with bias, it's our own shortcomings. Still, all of us have the responsibility to try each day to create school cultures and classrooms that are challenging and engaging. It's the only way to prepare students for the wider world that awaits them.

Here's what I want to see when I visit a school and when the state officials visit mine:

- Children being affirmed as capable and also challenged to be their best selves.
- Schools, administrators, and teachers conveying high expectations and providing adequate support for all students.
- Students who are happy to be in class and happy to be making choices, learning, and growing.
- Adults who are invested in, attentive to, and connected with kids, content, and colleagues.
- An overall feeling of positivity and joy.

It is easy to view building and sustaining a positive classroom culture as a semi-important or lower-priority issue. But it is actually *very* important and urgent. The stakes are high in schools right now. Research has demonstrated a strong correlation among organizational culture, teacher retention, and student performance (American University School of Education, 2022). Joyful and healthy cultures are the foundation of successful learning environments, promoting effective teaching and creativity and building student resilience. Teachers love working in schools that are positive and happy places. Students love attending these schools. And here's the thing: there's a lot we can do to ensure that they do! In this chapter, I'll share what I've learned about setting up and sustaining a positive culture by addressing its three most important pillars: engagement, challenge, and joy (see Figure 3.1), and recommending a strategy for building each.

Engagement

Engagement requires attention and interest from *all parties* present, and in a classroom, this means the teacher and the students.

FIGURE 3.1

Focal Points for Building Engagement, Challenge, and Joy in the Classroom

Engagement	Challenge	Joy
• Collaboration • Student Voice	• High Expectations • Growth Mindset	• Sense of Belonging • Strong Relationships

Engaging classrooms evoke thought, participation, and learning. They spark interest, inspiring students to think, ask questions, and apply the concepts to their lives. Engaging classrooms are populated with students who understand the teacher's expectations, and they're a place where even the most successful students feel challenged, creative, and connected to the content and one another. Engaging classrooms drive *relationships*. They are filled with raised hands, hands-on activities, and active learning. They reward students not just for getting the *right* answer but also for making an *effort* to answer. And they all seem to have a strong focus on literacy, no matter the discipline. When you think about it, it makes sense that an engaging environment is built on communication and connection. For this reason, I advocate focusing on literacy—*reading, writing, speaking,* and *listening*—as a way to increase engagement.

Prioritizing literacy

Sometimes we forget how important literacy is and the power it has to expose students to the wider world and provide access to opportunities (Dickson & Nickelsen, 2022). In truth, literacy is the foundation to success across all subjects.

Children in high-needs communities are less likely than others to be exposed to a wide array of books at home before they enroll in school, but this can be true of students from all sorts of backgrounds, and it's another reason it's so important to be curious about the lives of our students. The work we do to find out what their real needs and interests are pays off when we know how to address those needs most effectively.

The communities in which our students live can also play an important role in closing literacy exposure gaps. A quick story: I spent my first year as a principal in a struggling elementary school in North Philadelphia. Reynolds Elementary was located in a high-poverty area of the city and served the infamous Blumberg Housing Projects. When I arrived back in 1999, we had lots of love from the community and our students' families but few books in our library. So, with the help of some amazing teachers (Mrs. Hensford, Ms. Gay, and Ms. Debrow, all of whom were crazy about kids and led some of the most engaging and challenging classrooms I had ever seen), I wrote a proposal to the Philadelphia Eagles to ask for support for our library. They said yes! The organization and its many partners donated hundreds of new and used books for our students to read and keep.

Throughout the United States, community partners like professional sports teams—and like the United Way, YMCA, Boys and Girls Clubs of America, and many more—have invested millions of dollars and lots of human capital in helping to address some of the gaps in literacy that exist as early as preschool. They can really be a blessing. The theme of community engagement and connection will come up repeatedly in this book, because I have seen over and over again just how important they are.

At Reynolds Elementary, we set a goal to develop a team that focused on literacy and books in the library and classrooms. And we accomplished that goal. Not only did we add books, but they were diverse books that focused on themes our students would recognize in their own culture but exposed them to characters, events, and settings far beyond the boundaries of North Philly.

How students benefit from a literacy culture

A culture of literacy isn't just about getting your students to read; it's about how reading, writing, and literacy are embedded in your daily learning routines and activities. *Illiteracy* is one of the major determining factors of a child's education. It significantly affects graduation rates. It keeps students working below grade level. Literacy is also a *socioeconomic* issue. Consider these statistics (Regis College, 2023):

- Forty-three percent of adults living in poverty have a low literacy level.
- About four in five students living in economically disadvantaged communities see their reading skills decrease over school breaks

and during the summer due to a lack of resources and access to books.

- Fewer resources create the opportunity gap. On the 2022 National Assessment of Educational Progress, more than *half* of Black 4th graders and 45 percent of Latino/Hispanic 4th graders score below basic in reading compared to 23 percent of white students.
- Over 70 percent of prison inmates in the United States cannot read above a 4th grade level. The National Assessment of Adult Literacy reports that more than two-thirds of students who cannot read proficiently by the end of 4th grade will end up incarcerated or living in poverty.

A lack of resources for literacy worsens these gaps. But you can fight back against this inequity by working to promote literacy and embed it in your classroom. A culture of literacy does more than set up your students for success; it also fights against inequity in our school systems.

Literacy is a human right. When you break past these barriers and advocate for a culture of literacy, you empower more than education—you empower students' health and ability to understand their well-being, seek solutions, and make informed choices for their mind and body. You increase their capacity to learn, understand, and connect with others. You open up academic and career opportunities for their future. You allow them to stay informed and involved in the community by understanding local politics, news, and issues. You expand their minds, boost their confidence, and increase their quality of life. Literacy isn't just about books or even reading; it's about strengthening our personal power to understand, grow, and take action in our own lives (Concern Worldwide, 2023).

Why diversity in books and stories is important

We must be intentional about the reading material we use to empower student literacy (and engagement) and select ones that reflect diverse races, ethnicities, cultures, and backgrounds. Books and stories can help our students to make sense of the world, but when the worlds that books show don't look like the world our students know, and when the characters, events, and themes have little connection to themselves or to their communities, that power is diminished.

Consider that in 1985, less than 1 percent of children's books featured Black characters. Over 30 years later, in 2019, that number had risen to 12 percent, which is more or less in line with the percentage of Black Americans, according to demographic data in the 2020 U.S. Census (Flannery, 2020). The same study reports that Asian representation in 2019 children's books was 9 percent (compared to 6.1% of the U.S. population share), but Native American/Alaska Native characters were somewhat underrepresented (featured in less than 1% of children's books published in 2019 but 2.9% of the population), and Latino/Hispanic characters were dramatically underrepresented (featured in only 6.3% of 2019 children's books despite a population rate of 18.7%).

We must do better. Diversity in books tears down stereotypes. It validates students and allows more of them to see themselves and make sense of their experiences. Exposing students to stories focused on a diverse range of characters promotes empathy and cultural awareness across communities, regardless of the student's race, ethnicity, or culture. But a culture of literacy won't develop by accident; you must create it, plan it, and make it happen. I can help with that!

Strategy 1: Develop and follow a literacy plan.

You don't need a whole new, complex (and expensive) program. You just need to take the time to meet and formulate an overall literacy plan. Include administrators and educators from different grade levels and subjects. Invite students and the community to attend, if appropriate. The goal is to understand the importance of literacy and take steps to intentionally empower it in your daily lessons and activities across classrooms.

Here are some ways to go about this:

- **Take stock, together.** Collaborate with fellow teachers to examine the literacy-supporting practices you are currently using. For example: Are students who are studying ancient Africa or ancient Greece in history reading books related to these topics in their ELA classes? What kind of books are in your classroom libraries? Are you and your students talking about books you read at home? Sharing with students that you are a reader, too, sets a powerful example and is a point of connection.

- **Build up your library.** Schools with strong libraries have higher reading scores, literacy skills, and graduation rates (Martinez, 2024). Libraries give students a safe space to learn, explore, and make sense of the world. Your school librarian is likely to be one of the most joyful and engaging people on your staff. They help bring books and literacy to life for students and teachers. You can make your classroom a library, too. Consider creating a reading corner with books for students to relax and spend quiet time in. Stock it with titles they can relate to.
- **Increase access and equity.** Make sure all students have access to books. Diversify your library with books on unique subjects and reading levels. Consider setting up databases, eBooks, and audiobooks to provide digital learning content. Get to know each student in your classrooms and what kind of access to books they have at home.
- **Celebrate reading!** Stress that reading is rewarding and fun. Bring the stories to life with hands-on applications and activities. Talk about what your students are reading at home and in the classroom. Visualize their experiences by creating a "reading wall," highlighting the books and reading progress they have made. Don't design for comparison but as celebration and motivation to read more.
- **Involve the community.** Host book drives, plan reading-centered events, and encourage community members to donate new or used books. Get them involved in what you're reading. Ask questions about their views on reading, access to books at home, and how you can help. Educate the community on the importance of literacy and how they can get involved.

Challenge

Creating safe and welcoming spaces for children does not mean making school "easy." Life is full of challenges, and if students never learn how to face a challenge head-on, they will struggle to find success at much of anything.

I am a fan of teaching students to reframe challenge as an opportunity, not a threat. After all, challenges are what allow us to grow and learn as individuals. And the kinds of challenges students face in a classroom can be overcome with proper support and perseverance; students should know that, but too few of them do! We must teach all students how to approach challenge without fear, how to get back up again when they fail, and how to press on when they fall short. I often tell students, "If you can look up, you can get up!" (They love my catchy lines and rhymes, even though they say they don't!) This is more than just a catchphrase, though; it gets to the important heart of resilience and a growth mindset.

A challenging classroom is engaging and relevant to the students' inner worlds. It's built on collaboration more than competition, and it's driven by questioning and the search for understanding. It aims at promoting independence and each student's ability to gain control over their own learning, actions, and outcomes. It's productive, transformative, and forward-moving.

Challenging classrooms require teachers to plan meaningful, relevant lessons that promote collaboration, perseverance, and inspire students to show up and believe in the best versions of themselves. When students focus on becoming their best, they can improve their self-esteem, embrace their struggles in school and life, and learn to overcome many obstacles.

The value of a growth mindset and resilience

I want to reiterate the value of communicating to students that challenge is good for them and that a challenging classroom is a "testing ground" where students should be making mistakes and learning from them. It should *not* be a place where students only feel welcome when they get the right answers. Classrooms are not a trophy case; they're a place for learning, and learning is a process.

When we guide our students through their mistakes and provide them with the support they need to succeed, we help them move away from the idea that someone is either smart or not, "good at school" or not, and toward a *growth mindset* (Dweck, 2006), the belief that talents, abilities, knowledge, and understandings (academic and otherwise) can be developed through practice, hard work, and dedication. Remember the power of the word *yet*. A student might say to you, "I don't understand this book." That's a finite conclusion, a dead end. Now, add a *yet* to the end of that sentence ... and think about everything that could come next:

I don't understand this book yet, **so I will ask more questions.**

I don't understand this book yet, **so I will research ideas and events that confuse me.**

I don't understand this book yet, **so I will compare notes with my reading partner.**

Developing a growth mindset is a matter of shifting away from absolute statements to create room for growth. A growth mindset ignites resilience. It builds self-esteem, not only in the sense that it increases a student's belief in their ability to achieve their goals but also in the sense that they believe in their ability to overcome challenges by learning from setbacks and staying in the fight.

When our chess team first began competing against other middle schools, I encountered a very serious problem: they won right away! With so much success coming so quickly, they began getting arrogant. Their mindset at the time: *Because we're naturally good, we don't need to practice.* That's an absolute statement. Where could they go from there? I arranged for them to compete against some high school teams so that they could learn how to lose—more specifically, so they could learn how to pick themselves up from a loss and apply the lessons a loss contains. Once they understood that they needed to work to succeed, they worked and got even better. They started defeating some high school teams and even won against a team from Bucknell University. Those same students went on to win a national chess championship. When Arnold Schwarzenegger came to visit our school and play chess with our kids, one of our female players, Denise Pickard, got the best of him. Arnold mentioned Denise by name in his foreword to my first book, *I Choose to Stay* (Thomas-EL, 2003). It's safe to say "The Terminator" never forgot that chess game!

Fostering a growth mindset

Fostering a growth mindset takes time and dedication, and the work begins with us—the teachers and school leaders shifting the way we see our *own* efforts and outcomes. For example, if you've gotten comfortable thinking of yourself as good at some aspects of teaching and not as good at others, sit with that. To what extent might it signal a fixed mindset rather than a growth one? Are you still setting goals, working through your mistakes, and taking challenge in stride? Are you refusing to give up when students act out, fall short, or don't respond to a lesson or activity the way you'd hoped they would? Focus on adding a *yet* and set an example.

If you are a principal or other school leader, you can promote the growth mindset culture necessary in challenging classrooms by establishing a vision in which all students are successful and important. Setting these kinds of norms early in the culture-building process makes it easier for teachers and students to become a part of the fabric of the community. It's a way for staff members to embrace and understand what is expected of them. Note, too, that a good social-emotional learning (SEL) program is likely to include activities designed to build resilience in the classroom and schoolwide.

I want to quickly address something about the teaching profession that has bothered me for years: the unwritten rule that new and inexperienced teachers shouldn't smile until November or December. The accepted "wisdom" (it deserves the scare quotes) is that students need to know that the teacher is in charge—and is not there to be nice or be a friend. I'm not sure where this idea came from, but the work teachers do to develop positive relationships, maintain mutual respect, and foster joy is a much better indicator that they are "in charge" than being cold to kids. *Good teachers want relationships with students, not power over them.*

What are other ways that good teachers foster a growth mindset in students? They seek to understand their students' hopes and dreams as well as the doubts and false beliefs that may be holding these students back. They connect learning in the classroom to students' lives and give students opportunities to apply what they know and can do for their own benefit and the benefit of others. *Great teachers* do this as well—and also set high expectations for all students; when a teacher has a growth mindset, they know there's always something to try after every *yet*. They work continuously to hone their professional skills and provide students with the targeted support necessary to meet high expectations. *Amazing teachers* do all of the above, plus talk openly about the power of resilience. This leads us to another strategy.

Strategy 2: Normalize difficulty, encourage productive struggle, and celebrate progress.

Too many teachers make a habit of only rewarding student success. While we ought to recognize and celebrate our students' successes, we must *also* acknowledge that it takes struggle and difficulty to get there. So stress to your students that facing difficulty and getting a poor result doesn't mean they've failed—in fact, it's a part of the journey to success!

Here is my recommended approach:

- **Teach and encourage students to embrace their struggles.** Create a classroom culture that normalizes failures and setbacks, recognizes that struggle can be necessary, and rewards risk taking. Consider holding a short daily or weekly classroom community meeting to celebrate both wins and struggles. Get in the habit of reminding students that hard work beats talent every day of the year and that struggle is a huge part of success. Highlight their strengths and how they have grown over the weeks or months. Encourage them to embrace that learning is a journey and not a destination. I always saw myself as a cheerleader for growth when I was a teacher: the inspiration and voice of support students needed to help them cross the finish line.

- **Create multiple pathways to productive struggles and learning.** Teach students there are different paths to attaining success and to finding the right solution to a problem. Communicate to them that struggle and mistakes are expected parts of learning. Create rubrics and criteria for success so that they can see how they are approaching the learning goals.

- **Be honest about the level of difficulty of the lesson and set goals with students.** Don't avoid the hard problems or sugarcoat the lesson for students. Be honest and open about the challenges and obstacles they may face in your classroom. Try to phrase the challenge as a "not yet" problem: *You are **not yet** able to master this problem, but you will be when we are finished.* Develop goals and strategies with your students so they become comfortable with the challenges and difficulties of the lessons. It may be difficult in the beginning, but students will adapt with the appropriate, differentiated support.

We must begin to *challenge all students* at high levels so that they will know that high achievement is *possible for all students*. This is what Carol Ann Tomlinson calls "teaching up" (Tomlinson, 2023). Our expectations must be rooted in the belief that hard work and appropriate support will determine a child's success in school—not zip codes, not past academic record, not the language spoken at home, not household income. Differentiating instruction and giving students clear and authentic feedback are two ways we can make this belief a reality. So are developing growth mindsets and maintaining an engaging classroom environment.

Joy

People sometimes romanticize childhood as a care-free time, but educators know the truth: children navigate difficult emotions every hour of every day. Their homes and communities may not always be places of joy, but we can make their classroom one. And in doing so, we increase the odds that they will associate learning with a positive experience.

Joyful classrooms amplify students' voices and recognize their efforts. They are places that celebrate the curiosity, excitement, and satisfaction that come with learning, growth, and productivity. They encourage friendship and don't condone bullying, isolation, or embarrassment. They take the shame out of making mistakes and frame the learning process as a journey full of ups and downs. You see, joy isn't the same as happiness, and it's not about the ability to "avoid the bad." It's about finding or creating the good, *despite* the bad (Jaffe, 2021).

Fostering a culture of joy

Promoting joy in our schools can feel difficult in this age of high-stakes testing and accountability, yet there's joy at the heart of every positive and successful school. Joy comes from celebrating the small wins (moving up one level or adding 100 points to a previous score) along with the big ones (moving a student or the majority of the class to proficiency). It comes from knowing and celebrating students for who they are and all that they are (even if they're not on the honor roll). It comes from providing them with learning materials that resonate with them, inspire them, and delight them. It comes from framing the experience of learning as a group adventure rather than a solo task, even when students are working individually. And it comes through little things like bookending the time teachers and students spend together with routines of joy: helping students find connections to their own lives and the learning; sharing our love for music and reading with the kids; or just simply finding ways to show them the importance of being thankful, being happy, and showing gratitude. In short, joyful classrooms are all about *relationships*—students' stable and sustaining connection with the content, with the learning space, with one another, and with their teacher.

Joyful school cultures are built by sustaining effective relationships and consistency. Consistent adults in classrooms and schools are critical to developing authentic relationships and learning spaces. Children will adjust their behaviors according to expected consequences. This means that all adults must be consistent and undeviating in their responses to student conduct and choices. Students can and will participate and engage in learning more effectively when they clearly understand the classroom procedures and their importance. The teacher is the lead facilitator of classroom norms and expectations, and the principal is the prime facilitator of school culture and norms. Together, they are responsible for implementing classroom and school structures and providing guidance for holding students accountable for their behavioral choices. Teachers who make an impact and build positive relationships deliver clear and direct instructions and answer students' questions about expectations with clear feedback. Modeling and positive behavior incentives are great ways for educators to build positive classroom cultures, because truly, classroom culture starts with *us* (Gilmore, 2017).

Strategy 3: Prioritize students— their needs, challenges, and goals.

Our classrooms are a home away from home. For some students, they may be the best model of an organized, functional, and welcoming place they know. We want students to enter every classroom with the thought that someone took the time to create this special environment for them as a place where they are free to learn and grow. The keyword in that last sentence is *learn*. Growth is important, but learning (acquiring new knowledge, skills, and understandings) is what feeds human curiosity and spurs us to grow (do new things, take new risks, treat ourselves and others differently than we did before).

Here are some ways to prioritize students:

- **Encourage students to embrace curiosity, creativity, and growth.** This might include
  - Encouraging students to ask deeper questions (teach them how, if necessary), read as much as possible, and delve as deeply as they want to into aspects of the curriculum that interest them.
  - Introducing songs, dance, and music into your lessons, or take energizing breaks to move and stretch while listening to *their* favorite songs.
  - Steering students toward books that reflect their lives and experiences and encouraging them to write their own stories about their own lives.
  - Creating corners in the classroom where students can play chess, sudoku, Scrabble, Wordle, and other thinking games.
  - Regularly acknowledging students' potential, growth, and success—especially in situations where you see them pursuing their interests, taking risks, and becoming more comfortable with their authentic selves.
- **Make sure your students are at the heart of your school's and classroom's design.** Think about
  - Making decor colorful and interactive.
  - Making sure the school playground has equipment the students enjoy and (space permitting) quiet spaces for students with sensory issues; modified walkways and slides for maximum accessibility; and possibly even areas for musical instruments with connections to the students' culture. There needs to be safety padding or mulch to soften any falls.
  - Decorating classrooms, hallways, and communal spaces with as much teacher- and student-generated work as possible.
  - Using (or encourage the use of) flexible seating, which promotes engagement and focus during class (Minero, 2015) and reduces discipline issues and referrals (Merrill, 2017).

- **Create opportunities to find joy while recognizing the challenges and struggles of teaching and learning.** The joy of learning and feeling seen and heard in schools keeps students coming back each day. In challenging times, students (and teachers too) yearn for safe spaces where they are heard and valued. You might try
  - Scheduling "office hours." This is time for teachers to sit down and listen to students share their perspective on school-related challenges, the joyfulness of school, or whatever else is on their minds during a morning advisory period, at lunchtime, or after school.
  - Acknowledging the challenges your teachers are facing (this one is for administrators!) and presenting yourself as a partner ready to help them rediscover the joy in it. A positive school environment is a draw for good teachers and a must for keeping them in your school building.
  - Creating and promoting joyful before- and after-school events that bring faculty and families together, like "Donuts with Grownups," celebrations, readings, poetry, workshops, pizza night, and so on. This gets parents knocking the door down to *get into* the school instead of knocking the door down to get out.

Reflect & Take Action

A study of Chicago Public Schools found that a strong sense of connectedness between teachers and students was *more* impactful on how safe a student felt than the crime rates and poverty levels in their district (Steinberg et al., 2011). National data also show these positive teacher-student relationships help to decrease behavioral issues in school and support more student engagement. Many cities and states recognize the importance of connections, student engagement, and the development of social-emotional skills. Effective and successful programs that focus on equity and relationships prioritize the implementation of SEL, communication, and relationship-building strategies.

Again, the best teachers and administrators know that our students' success will be impacted by our ability to build and sustain positive relationships with them and their families (Kaufman, 2024).

Reflection questions

Take a moment to reflect on Chapter 3 and how it applies to your unique district, school, classroom, and students. Consider:

1. In what ways is your school or classroom engaging?
2. In what ways is your school or classroom challenging?
3. In what ways is your school or classroom joyful?
4. How can you (on your own and with colleagues) inspire a culture of literacy for your students?
5. What steps are you taking to help students to see themselves and their families reflected in the classroom? Does your room welcome all learners and foster a sense of safety and belonging? Try using the checklist in Figure 3.2 to take stock.
6. What are some things you could do to develop a growth mindset for yourself *and* model it for your students?

FIGURE 3.2
Classroom Diversity and Inclusion Checklist

Classroom Diversity and Inclusion Checklist

☐ Books, texts, and other resources that reflect the diversity and cultures of the students in the classroom

☐ Books, texts, and other resources at various reading levels

☐ Books, texts, and other resources of various types and genres: leveled readers, graphic novels, audiobooks

☐ Books, texts, and other resources in students' home languages, along with dual-language dictionaries and other learning aids to support language development

☐ Flexible seating arrangements and "time-out" space for self-selected retreat

☐ Lessons, assignments, and assessment differentiated based on readiness, interest, and learning preferences

Next steps

True change requires action. Empower the bigger picture by working on long-term goals:

- Intentionally design and redesign your school and classrooms around your students' needs each year and semester.
- Form a literacy leadership team.
- Take steps to ensure your students feel welcome, safe, and intellectually challenged in the classroom all year.

4

Critical Thinking Skills

When Shanea Higgin, a member of our chess team, received a permission slip to travel to the Elementary National Chess Championship in Dallas, Texas, in May 2014, she was surprised she'd made the cut. You see, just two months before, we'd competed at the Junior High Championship in Atlanta, and Shanea hadn't done too well. She was an amazing 6th grader and an awesome young lady. She was a good student, too; I don't think Shanea Higgin ever received a grade lower than an *A* in any class the entire time she was with us at Thomas Edison Charter School. The only time she seemed to struggle at all was when she was playing chess.

Shanea was determined. She came to every chess practice and every match. She was also reserved and soft-spoken, and that affected her performance in matches against the more aggressive players, especially the boys. Once in a while, though, she would win against one of the older guys, and she would celebrate. We all would! But because Dallas was a plane ride away and the National Elementary Chess Tournament would stretch over three days, we couldn't afford to bring the entire chess team. Shanea was not on my list of 10 competitors.

Actually, we originally had no plans at all to compete as a team in Dallas, because we were short on the funds necessary to cover hotel rooms, flights, and meals. But then I spoke at an educational conference in San Antonio, telling stories about our school and chess team, and one of the attendees walked up to me afterward and handed me a check. I said thanks without looking at the total and placed it in my shirt pocket. (I've lost count of the number of times people hearing about our chess team have handed me a check for $20, even $50. But this time was different.) Another attendee encouraged me to take a second look at the check, and when I did, I almost passed out. Twenty *thousand* dollars? This was the largest personal check I had ever seen in my life! The donor turned out to be a hugely successful commercial real estate agent, who later communicated with us that she preferred to remain anonymous, and so she has. I called my office staff and announced, "We're going to Nationals! Let the kids know!"

We were on a tight timeline, so our staff sprang into action. I gave them the names of the 10 chess players I'd identified to make the trip so that permission slips could be printed and sent home. Soon after, when I spotted Shanea during dismissal, I prepared myself to explain to her why she wouldn't be making the trip to Dallas with us. But Shanea was smiling as she approached me. Her words also came as a surprise: "Thanks for the permission slip. I didn't think I would be going!" As neutrally as I could, I asked Shanea if she really received a trip slip, and she said yes. *Oh, someone made a mistake,* I thought. I didn't have the courage to ask for the slip back, so I told Shanea to have a nice evening. Turns out, my assistant principal Liz Yates had added Shanea to the list; she'd assumed I had made a mistake by leaving her off! "No worries," I told Liz. "Let's take Shanea. It will be a fun experience for her, even if she does not do well."

As it turned out, our students *did* do well in the tournament, placing near the top of our section each day until the next-to-last round, where most of them lost their games. We still had a chance to take the top prize, but *everyone* needed to win in the 7th and final round. That didn't happen. But unexpectedly, Shanea got a draw in her final match, and the half-point it earned was enough to secure us a tie for first place. *Shanea Higgin was our hero!* Without her, we wouldn't have brought home the prize. The parade and big welcome waiting for us were amazing. We told Shanea's story of resilience to everyone, and our entire community embraced her as a champion. Her persistence, critical thinking skills, and creativity allowed her to play chess at her highest level and when the competition was the toughest. After graduating from Thomas Edison Charter School, Shanea Higgin went on to a great high school. She's currently a scholarship student at the University of Delaware.

I wanted to tell this story here, at the beginning of a chapter focused on the value of teaching critical thinking to students, for a couple of reasons. First, I think educators need reminders that on those days when we are really feeling the weight of our responsibilities, some hardworking, thoughtful, positive kid like Shanea will walk up to just to say hi or to say, "You helped me so much," and their beautiful energy will instantly remind us that what we do is worth the stress. Being "crazy about kids" is being elated for and about them, and about all they do and are capable of doing. The best compensation for our work is the joy they bring us and the satisfaction we get from being trusted to support their cognitive, social, and emotional development. This is a far more complex responsibility than a high-stakes test could ever assess, but an educator's work is far more complex than getting kids to master content standards and memorize facts!

Although thinking critically and creatively are important 21st century skills, there are many children still attending schools where memorization is the foundation of most lessons. For educators who are crazy about kids, this won't do! When we truly care about our students, we look for ways to support the development of their brains. Supportive relationships, consistent and productive critical thinking exercises, and positive communication all do that (Siegel & Bryson, 2012). It's why I started teaching chess to students, and it's why I always think about our chess teams and chess players, like Shanea, when the topic turns to critical thinking.

Critical thinking and brain capacity develop most when children feel emotionally and physically safe, connected, engaged, joyful, and challenged. When educators are also curious about the lives of our students, when we adopt a culture of high expectations and loving support, we position them to grow into their greatest potential. Yes, we're back to the Four Cs! If you use the Four Cs to guide your practice, you, too, will discover ways to connect with students and push them to develop both their cognitive skills and very important life skills, like self-discipline and self-motivation. We must *engage* them before we inform them, *reach* them before we can teach them.

If chess is not for you, something else could serve the same purpose. I've also used strategic sports (basketball, tennis), games (Sudoku,

Scrabble), and other activities to connect with students and tap into their interests. This is the engagement they need so that information can take root, and it is such a powerful force! You can use almost any activity that will keep the kids engaged; the only requirement is that aspects of the activity connect to the lesson and targeted learning outcomes.

About Critical Thinking

Chess is a game of problem solving. It teaches those who play it to think ahead—to find a solution to a problem that hasn't even *happened* yet. It also teaches patience through abstract reasoning and out-of-the-box thinking; the average chess game has about 40 moves, each made thoughtfully and strategically. Chess also encourages players to find patterns, learn from past mistakes, and continually improve. It teaches them to focus on the present moment while *still* planning ahead (Martin, 2021).

This is the heart of critical thinking: the ability to analyze evidence, create connections, and evaluate solutions. It's the ability to think logically, build hypotheses, and understand information in a balanced, rational way. It's the type of reasoning we use to ask questions, find answers, and, most important, apply these answers to challenges facing us in our lives. Critical thinking bridges the gap between the classroom and the "real world." It encourages students to take what they've learned from books, lessons, and assignments and connect it with their everyday lives (Delamain & Spring, 2020).

In short, instruction in critical thinking and opportunities to practice it prepare students to think for themselves and find understanding rather than just catalog facts and memorize correct responses. This should be a primary goal for all educators. However, as reported by The Reboot Foundation (2018, 2020), multiple surveys revealed the following:

- Nearly 22 percent of U.S. adults feel it's a child's *own* responsibility to learn critical thinking; over 40 percent believe it's the responsibility of primary and secondary school teachers.
- Only 39 percent of U.S. 8th grade teachers surveyed reported emphasizing critical thinking skills, such as deductive reasoning, in the classroom.

- Forty-one percent of teachers believe students should be taught critical thinking *during* their lessons; 42 percent of teachers believe students should be taught basic facts first, *then* critical thinking; 16 percent believe the two should be taught separately.
- More than *half* of teachers feel standardized testing gets in the way of teaching critical thinking.

When it comes to critical thinking, we're not on the same page, whether as parents, teachers, or educators. I'll make my position clear, though: unless more teachers teach their students to develop reasoning skills and make creative connections, these students will continue to struggle in school and life.

Yes, students are struggling. They're struggling to think on their own, learn on their own, and make decisions on their own. Critical thinking skills are what empower our students to turn problem solving into an intentional process; they're how students know to ask questions about what they *already* know and what they *need* to know to make the best decision. These skills are also key to knowing whether or not a decision is a good decision or the *best* decision. Students with strong critical thinking skills have the perspective they need to make logical judgments and find success when there's *not* a teacher or parent around to tell them what to do.

What else does critical thinking help students do? It helps them set goals and identify the facts. It helps them pinpoint a problem, brainstorm solutions, and then examine the possible solutions and determine which one to try. In this way, critical thinking is the heart of healthy independence. We should take the time to teach it now so that students can better support themselves in the future. I say this from the heart, because I have seen where critical thinking skills can take our kids.

A critical thinking success story

I met Nathan Durant when he was in middle school in Philadelphia. He had been homeschooled for most of his education and was struggling to make the transition to our school. I did my best to make a connection with him. Growing up in the inner city with no father around to help can take a toll on our young men, and Nate, who kept getting in fights, was an example of that.

One day, when Nate came in front of me for discipline, I offered to waive his school suspension if he joined the chess team. He agreed and went on to become one of our best players. It was clear early on that Nate had the makings of an excellent critical thinker and problem solver; with instruction in chess strategy, those skills grew stronger. He subsequently got involved in many activities in our school, including student government, the science and algebra clubs, and others. He realized that he loved solving puzzles and debating about any topic he could find. Nate's potential had been there all along; he just needed some guidance, direction, and time to develop. Nate went on to attend the High School for Engineering and Science in Philadelphia, one of the city's top magnet schools. He made that decision. He chose that challenging path for himself and went on to help his high school team win their first-ever City Chess Championship.

After graduation from Kutztown University in eastern Pennsylvania, Nate pursued a career in insurance sales and moved from job to job. On several occasions, he slept on our couch or in our basement, just to make ends meet. When he told me he was considering a teaching career and, later, approached me about helping out with the chess team at my school, I was all in. As a teaching assistant at Russell Byers Charter School in Philadelphia, where I was principal, Nate not only helped us build a winning chess team but also met his wife, who was one of our teachers. Today, they have two beautiful children.

Nate later joined me at my new school in Delaware. He earned a master's degree and a teaching certification. Along with another of my former students, Thomas Allen, he became an integral part of our chess coaching team. Nate is now a principal at a nearby high school in Wilmington. I'm tremendously proud of him for all he has overcome and accomplished. I am grateful for the relationship we've built. And I trace it back to him being open to learning chess and developing the critical thinking and growth mindset that has powered his success.

A hidden benefit: Critical thinking as character-building

Critical thinking inspires application. It encourages students to internalize the ideas and content they encounter and do something with them! It's a key component of experiential learning, active learning, and social-emotional learning. But one very important benefit of critical thinking often goes under the radar: the way it *builds character*. Let me explain.

Our students' minds are constantly active, taking in and processing countless amounts of new information each day. Because of this, students often make decisions and judgments without consciously thinking them through. But critical thinking puts *them* in control. It encourages their thought processes to be active, not just reactive. It gives them more accountability for their actions. It urges them to think, *"Is this the best thing I could do or say in this situation?"* It inspires ethical reasoning, inviting them to make sound judgments and choices that build character.

These critical thinking skills are a *necessity*. I've seen that when schools are driven by the needs of their teachers, students, and families—not just by the curriculum standards or standardized test scores—staff and student joy increase. Student engagement becomes visible in every aspect of the school. Children have an innate curiosity and benefit from learning environments that lean into exploration and discovery. Students who feel supported and challenged are eager to explore the world around them and learn as much information as possible. They are not afraid to make mistakes or fail when learning, which builds character and resilience they'll take with them moving forward. When the school culture does not focus on the emotional well-being, resilience, or character of the students, their natural love for school can become lost. Fortunately, the love of learning, critical thinking, and creativity can be quickly developed and nurtured in a culture of love and high expectations.

Strategies for Empowering Critical Thinking

If we are serious about investing in building cultures of critical thinking, character, and life-long success, we must take immediate and swift action so our staff and students know it is a priority. Promote learning for all and collaboration together with one another. Celebrate diversity and build meaningful relationships. These actions will all send an *immediate* message that you are focusing on thinking critically, on creativity, and on relationships, not just test scores. Fostering caring and productive relationships with parents and kids is huge when developing a supportive learning environment and making connections with the home and community. To solidify these efforts, educators must promote effective strategies for teaching critical thinking and other social and emotional skills among staff members.

So how do we teach our students to think for themselves? How can we empower critical thinking in our classrooms? Remember: we must engage *before* we inform. This leads to the first strategy for empowering critical thinking.

Strategy 1: Jumpstart critical thinking through creative play.

The adolescent brain is unique, creative, and curious. It's developed and shaped by consistent, supportive relationships. Children who attend schools with a positive culture, where they can feel physically and emotionally safe, are able to improve their brain's capacity to process information (Darling-Hammond & Cook-Harvey, 2018). They need a learning environment where they feel safe to take risks, ask questions, volunteer answers, and take part—one where they can make mistakes and *still* feel comfortable trying again. When we foster the curiosity and creativity of the brain, students can develop confidence, resourcefulness, and resilience.

Students can learn to think critically and solve problems through the process of playing games that are well-planned, linked to the curriculum, and thoughtfully integrated into the lesson. But there is also value in adding some games to the beginning or end of a lesson to give students a "brain break" from the academic pressures of school (even though, as noted, even these just-for-fun games help to build cognitive power) and to get positive and joyful energy flowing. Incorporating games and activities with skill-related components, like puzzles and Sudoku, are a way to capture and hold students' attention, turning practice from drudgery to fun. Research shows that increased focus, practice, and time on-task are particularly important for students who struggle in school. Games also create opportunities for students to collaborate, boost class participation, and can foster social and emotional learning and motivate students to take risks. Critical thinking and problem-solving games and activities teach students to make quick decisions and analyze their consequences in a low-pressure setting. These lessons are valuable for students, not only in school but in life (Farber, 2021). Figure 4.1 lists a number of games and activities that promote critical thinking and problem solving.

FIGURE 4.1
Games and Activities That Promote Critical Thinking

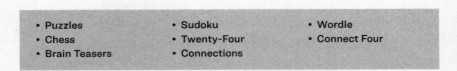

- Puzzles
- Chess
- Brain Teasers
- Sudoku
- Twenty-Four
- Connections
- Wordle
- Connect Four

As you know, my game of choice for students is chess. It's a game that students can study and play alone or with others. It's a game that teaches patience under pressure and trains players to use problem-solving skills to decide which pieces to move and when to move them. Chess requires players to wait for their opponent's move, then scan the entire chess board for potential moves and outcomes. Visualizing what will happen with each possible move and then quickly coming up with new moves in real time requires and reinforces creative and critical thinking (Whitby School, n.d.). In addition to building students' critical thinking and problem-solving skills, chess asks players to identify assumptions and ideas. This boosts their ability to make good decisions and interact constructively with others.

Learning is very social, emotional, and internal. By engaging before we inform, we warm up their critical thinking skills. We ease them into the lesson, building connections, not just between the data and principles, but with *each other* as teachers and students. When we build connections and engage with students, we are showing that we value them and that we are curious about their lives and their learning, both in school and outside in the community. Students must feel safe in the space to engage and be present. They must feel comfortable with their teachers and fellow classmates. Find challenging yet approachable activities that segue into your lessons, encourage collaboration, and reward participation.

Strategy 2: Provide positive decision-making experiences.

In a standard classroom Q&A scenario, the teacher asks the question and the student answers. Encourage critical thinking by flipping the script! By that, I mean try planning lessons that challenge students to ask questions and make decisions themselves. Allow them the freedom to express curiosity and apply what they've learned. Design activities where they must evaluate the "pros and cons" of a decision, evaluating the best solution available.

I recommend the *explore-before-explain* method (Ferlazzo, 2021):

- **First, ask students to *explore*.** Give your students a chance to review the information themselves. Work backward, letting them see the answers and generate their own questions. This ties perfectly into our "engage before you inform" approach! Giving them the freedom to explore and make sense of the evidence *first* allows them to engage, ask questions, and prepare their minds for learning. Invite your students to guess the *why* and the *how*. Let them investigate the situation, share their reasoning, and make their own predictions.

- **Then, ask students to *explain*.** In this stage, students connect their answers and guesses to the core principles of the assignment. Recognize their efforts and let students explain and make sense of the assignments, readings, and discussions (Brown, 2023).

This exercise can inspire your students to become teachers—of themselves, of peers, and maybe, someday, as a career! It encourages them to know the *why* of the "right answer," not just the *what* of it.

Strategy 3: Encourage new perspectives, collaboration, and teamwork.

Show students how to explore concepts from multiple perspectives by taking the time to break down different ways to approach and solve problems. The aim is to show them the process of forming well-rounded opinions and encourage them not to just accept without question someone else's answer or solution. Here are some ways to do this:

- **Model critical analysis and decision making.** Providing concrete guidance in critical analysis is more effective than hoping students will pick it up on their own. This can be done as early as the early years of elementary school and as late as high school. At the elementary level, discussion might center on a book or story students are hearing read aloud or reading themselves. Elementary teachers can also lead conversations about basic decisions we have to make, like what to do this weekend or the best way to spend $10. In the secondary or upper grades, teachers can teach varying kinds of reasoning in their lessons or kick off lessons with short activities focused on logic. Teachers in my school have found that using various resources, like documentaries and articles on historical figures, is the key to engaging older students. Inviting guest speakers to share their experiences in class or creating an activity highlighting, say, deductive reasoning when reading *The Hound of the Baskervilles* in 9th grade English are great ways to teach decision making and critical thinking to adolescents.
- **Embrace teamwork.** Dividing students into groups for projects and discussions not only fosters collaboration and compromise but also exposes students to diverse perspectives, gives them practice communicating with others about academic ideas, and gives them chances to teach and learn from others. When students learn from others through discussions and debates, it promotes critical thinking and challenges them to become better decision-makers. Also, as they develop their communication skills through collaboration, they will develop a deeper understanding of the subjects they are studying and appreciate their peers more. With deeper appreciation comes empathy, which I regard as a necessary life skill.
- **Mix up your instructional approaches.** Give students opportunities to tackle problems and assignments as group members and individuals. They need to practice thinking independently *and* as a team. Using an inquiry-based model unlocks the curiosity of students and allows them to be creative when thinking critically. Remember to encourage students to develop their own questions and find the answers on their own whenever they can and not rely

too heavily on their team. This is the most effective way to develop their curiosity and self-directed learning.

- **Diversify resources to offer varying viewpoints.** Many schools are full of students who are exposed to a single academic perspective (e.g., the textbook's) or only perspectives that align with those of the teacher. Asking students to take in a variety of perspectives on literature, history, and current events is enriching. It's a way to boost their awareness of others' authentic experiences and broaden their horizons. Yes, achievement gaps are necessary targets for educators, but exposure gaps are too! When we challenge students to consider new and different points of view, we encourage open-mindedness, which has tremendous value in analysis and problem solving.

Strategy 4: Ask for *whys* and *hows*, not just *whats*.

The world is full of opinions, perspectives, and solutions; the ability to analyze them and determine which is the "right" one or which is best in which circumstances is one of the most valuable skills a student can develop. As noted, educators can help facilitate this by modeling the process and calling out each step of analysis. We can also ask more open-ended questions to welcome deeper reflection and individualized application.

For example, if you divide the class into five different groups to brainstorm a solution to such a problem, even when given the same resources and guidance, each group will likely come up with a unique response. Review each group's solution, acknowledging their creativity and critical thinking. Then compare and contrast each group's approach and ask *them* to walk you through their solution-finding process. Tell them that you're interested in why they generated the solution that they did. Explain that you want to know *how* they got from Point A to Point B.

What about in situations where there *is* a definitive right or best answer? When your students get the right answer, ask them to explain it. The act of doing so helps them remember the process and do it again. It helps them make better sense of the answer *and* their reasoning. It can also help them understand and view the concept in new ways.

When your students get the wrong answer, direct them toward finding the "missing piece" in their reasoning. Prompt them to retrace their steps to see where and understand why they made a "wrong turn"; from there, provide support (through prompts and questions) so they can find their way back to the right answer. Oftentimes, you can do this by simply asking students to rethink their responses or to try to relate the task to current events and real-world experiences. Then watch their faces light up when they see different pathways to the correct answer. Another way to encourage students to think critically about how they arrived at an answer is to ask them the question in a different way, see if their response changes, and then dig into why.

By the way, when students are prompted to rethink a wrong answer, they will likely discover they weren't completely "wrong"; even if the ultimate response was incorrect, some of their reasoning was likely creative and on track! Recognize this and make sure they recognize it, too!

How Critical Thinking Fits into a Four Cs Mindset

Creating a safe, secure space for students to share their reasoning, whether correct or incorrect, fosters an environment for deeper, lasting learning. It lets students know it's *OK* to participate. It's *OK* to make mistakes. It's *OK* to be heard. Normally, students who are confident in the right answer are the first to raise their hands. But by asking deeper, more reflective questions and normalizing the making of mistakes, we can spark broader engagement and participation. As we consistently create a safe space for everyone, we can empower *critical thinking for all.*

Adults who are consistently crazy and curious about their students create safe spaces for young people and help them develop routines that empower those same students to have a sense of security. This safety and security are the consistency our students need. We can achieve this simply through modeling, planning, organizing schedules, and designing the learning environment for *consistent* success. Learning problem-solving skills and critical thinking in a supportive and loving school culture allows children to resist peer pressure, make good decisions, and form their own opinions in school and in life. When teachers and parents can get students accustomed to a routine and a consistent schedule, the children also learn that there are activities in life we schedule that may not be fun but are necessary and must be accomplished. Dealing with change is an important part of life. Critical thinking is just as important for students as it is for adults, and it is vital that we model these skills. We can teach students to solve problems and think reflectively through our actions and words.

Children don't always get to determine how their day goes or control their circumstances. They are typically expected to roll with the punches and overcome obstacles while the adults try to keep them safe, happy, warm, and fed. Clear structure, procedures, and expectations teach self-discipline, character, and self-reliance. They provide limits and boundaries that help children predict how parents and other adults will react to their behaviors. Our consistency as educators and leaders will allow them the freedom to make mistakes, think outside the box, and develop the character that critical thinking truly empowers.

Reflect & Take Action

In the standard teacher-student classroom relationship, the teacher defines the right answer and process, and the student accepts it. Students aren't often encouraged to ask why that's the right answer and process; they're usually told to get on board with it because it's right. Yet, this approach can stifle curiosity and creativity.

Critical thinking urges us to reexamine the relationships we have with our students and their comfort in safely discussing, brainstorming, and analyzing a problem back and forth with authority figures. By putting consistent, healthy relationships at the forefront, we can teach students to think critically and carefully. Students who face trauma and stress on a regular basis can truly benefit from good critical thinking skills. They lead to better relationships with adults, less stress, and increased happiness in life.

Reflection questions

Take a moment to reflect on Chapter 4 and how it applies to your unique district, school, classroom, and students. Consider:

1. How can you support and encourage critical thinking in your school or classroom?
2. How would your students benefit from critical thinking skills?
3. What are the main barriers to teaching critical thinking in your school or classroom?
4. How might you overcome these barriers?
5. How could you make your school or classroom a safer space for students to explore and grow their critical thinking skills?

Next steps

True change requires action. Empower the bigger picture by working on long-term goals:

- At the beginning of the school year, invite your students to help you create the classroom rules. Ask questions about the *why* and *how*, not just the *what*.
- Keep an ongoing record of your students' evolving interests. Find ways to jumpstart their critical thinking by incorporating relevant activities connected to these interests.
- Encourage critical thinking in your classroom by flipping the script. Plan lessons that challenge students to ask deeper questions and make decisions themselves. Allow them the freedom and safe space to express curiosity and apply what they've learned.

5

After-School Programs and Community Engagement

During lunch at a suburban restaurant outside Philadelphia, the waiter stopped by our table several times to comment on how much fun we seemed to be having and how we must all be really good friends. I confirmed that we were, adding that we'd known one another for a very long time—almost 30 years!

The men I had lunch with that day were Shawn, Rodney, and Dante. I introduced them earlier in this book. They're former students of mine whom I taught in the early days of my career, before I had really started focusing on developing my chess program. I actually coached these guys on the basketball team, and it was an adventure, to say the least. Shawn took more shots than Allen Iverson, Dante always thought he was a better coach and player than I was, and Rodney was Charles Barkley and Shaquille O'Neal rolled into one. I absolutely loved these young men back in the day, and I love them now.

Although I formed an initial relationship with Shawn, Rodney, and Dante during the school day, in our in-school suspension program, it really blossomed in the after-school basketball program. Before long, we expanded our basketball team activities and started playing open games on Saturday mornings, inviting members of the community to join in. Attorneys, teachers, politicians, utilities company employees, and airport employees all came out to play ball with the kids. Other students, family members, and adult mentors would cheer them on. We all had break-fast together after those Saturday games, and the conversations we had around the table generated invitations to other events, like workshops on applying to college and starting a business. Eventually, these gatherings evolved into a Saturday tutoring group. My mother cooked for these kids every weekend while she was alive, and those amazing meals might have been the reason so many of them never missed a tutoring session!

After high school, Rodney and Shawn attended and finished college together at Cheyney University, which is the oldest Historically Black College (HBCU) in the nation. (HBCU graduates debate this topic all the time; some argue that Lincoln University, also in Pennsylvania, is actually the first.) Dante attended Philadelphia Community College for a short time and built both a family and a wonderful career at Wachovia Bank. He eventually finished his college degree at Strayer University in 2014, making good on a promise he had made to himself. All of us—his former teachers and family—were very proud of him. He has inspired us further with his resilience by beating kidney cancer—not once but twice, in 2015 and 2017.

Lunch that day was possible because of a decision I had made early in my career about what relationships would mean to me as an educator: they would be the foundation for everything in my classroom and beyond. Over the years, Shawn, Rodney, and Dante have all told me that my influence on them was powerful and that they consider me something of a father figure. Every educator understands how validating comments like that are. They mean so much. Being this kind of positive force in our students' lives, playing a role of lasting significance, is something many of us strive for, and it's a challenging milestone to reach. We want to get kids to succeed in school, but we also want to help them develop qualities and attitudes that last and can guide them long after they have left our classrooms.

How do we establish authentic connections and relationships with students in a way that serves them long term? How can we leverage best practices with students to form better relationships with school staff and other adults in the home and community? Many educators may try to focus on curriculum first, but the true road to becoming effective as an educator is to focus on establishing healthy and trusting relationships with students.

My relationship with Rodney, Dante, and Shawn didn't *begin* with them considering me a father figure. That took years of building and cultivating trust and connection. Both tough love and tough decisions were involved. But when I started to show interest in their lives outside school, they began trusting me more, and trust is the engine that drives meaningful relationships. Sure, our connection began in the classroom, but it really developed in our after-school programs.

After-School Programs as Opportunities

The Four Cs make it possible for all kinds of educators to create a sustained and consistent system of support for all kinds of kids. At the same time, every student needs to know that they are unique and incredible; just them being who they are brings us joy. This joy—this being crazy about them—sustains us as educators. It's why we commit ourselves long-term to our students' success and well-being. Within a joyful culture that promotes empathy and support, students can truly feel both that they belong (because they do) and that the adults around them are rooting for their success (because they are).

Working with students in after-school programs presents us with additional opportunities to help them to feel emotionally safe and appreciate just how crazy we are about them. This is also additional time for educators to learn about students' personalities, needs, and interests. We can apply the insights we gain to provide them with more effective scaffolds, identify and implement more personalized and effective approaches to engagement, and better support their social-emotional development.

I am so honored to have had the chance to mentor students and boost their sense of belonging over my near 40 years in education. But it wasn't just me; so many adults have contributed to the academic, social, and emotional success of my students through after-school programs. When kids feel a sense of safety and consistency in school, after school, at home, and in the community, it's easier for them to trust, easier to take risks, and easier to just exist! Bottom line: When we show students that we are crazy about them through an investment of time and attention beyond the school day, they feel valued and valuable. When the adults around them believe in them, students gain the courage they need to set and pursue goals and the confidence they need to reach their full potential.

Let's take a step back. Students spend 25 percent of their time in school (National Conference of State Legislatures, 2021). We might say that, as teachers and administrators, we know just one-quarter of their personalities and potential. Of course, it's easy to think it's just our job to worry about the 25 percent: we're there to teach at school, and that's it. But if we are truly going to lead the way to change in the educational system, we must think bigger. The majority of students' lives takes place outside school. We *cannot* ignore that what happens there affects their experience in the classroom. We *cannot* ignore the impact their home life, friends, and family have on their current reality and future outcomes.

As Sparks (2019) reports, a meta-analysis of 46 different studies measuring the short- and long-term outcomes of positive teacher-student relationships concluded that these relationships improve key factors we care about as teachers and administrators: student academic performance, engagement, and attendance. And they decrease the number of unwanted behaviors, suspensions, and dropout rates in schools. And it's not just about the *students*, either. The number one predictor of whether or not a teacher will have a joyful, positive job experience is the relationships that they have with their students (Sparks, 2019).

Building strong relationships with students begins with us, the *adults*, making an effort to connect with *them*. There are endless ways to do this as teachers, administrators, and classified school staff, including joining students at recess to play games, reading to and talking with students during lunch, creating roles for students in the classroom that support their ability to contribute meaningfully to a communal goal, and reaching out to families to share positive news. The relationships that develop from these connections boost children's ability to combat the stresses of school. They stimulate students' brains and motivate them to engage in the learning process. These relationships also help support students' emotional well-being, self-regulation, and motivation.

Building and maintaining these relationships takes effort from both parties. But as the teachers and leaders in the school, we can take an active role in this journey by participating in, advocating for, and supporting after-school programs.

Research shows after-school programs can increase students' academic outcomes, classroom attendance, and social-emotional learning (Turnbaugh, 2015). Consistent participation, and the sense of belonging that comes from well-run after-school programs, paves the way to higher graduation rates and smaller opportunity gaps.

The Keys to Building Good and Sustainable After-School Programs

Our school has academic after-school programs to assist students with reading and math fundamentals, but we also offer activities that focus on martial arts, tennis, and gardening. We even have a math program, Lyrical Math, that taps into our students' love of hip-hop and rap music. Academic success is important, but we also pay close attention to the emotional well-being of the students and staff. Remembering how essential consistency is, we find outside partners and local universities to provide additional teachers, tutors, and adult sponsors so we don't overwork our staff, who are already doing so much and under lots of stress.

The research is clear that high-quality after-school programs can transform our students' experiences and outcomes. However, there is a major *if:* these positive effects occur only if the programs are of high quality. To unlock the considerable benefits of after-school programs, I recommend focusing on the following elements:

- **Scheduling and leadership.** After-school programs must be consistent and frequent. They must be led by trained staff members who understand the program's purpose and goals. It's the responsibility of administrators and district leaders to provide teachers with the training and support to facilitate these activities effectively.
- **Clear goals and objectives.** The overall mission of the after-school program at our school, Thomas Edison, is to improve students' academic and social/life skills and boost their success in class and in the community. A daily goal is to offer a safe and healthy environment that enriches our kids' lives. We want to provide them with more support but also more joy. Setting and monitoring objectives for each individual program can promote consistency and effectiveness. In our chess program, for example, our goal is to develop the critical

thinking and problem-solving skills of each student, along with character and resilience. We also seek to help our students develop interpersonal skills and learn to be kind to others when competing.

- **Support from community partners.** Teachers and staff don't have to lead these programs alone, and it's often better if they don't! Bringing in community support is a way to access more funding and adult leaders. A little targeted outreach to parents, families, and community pillars about the value of after-school programs (and details on how they might get involved) should be a part of your plan.

- **Opportunities for social-emotional development.** After-school programs are a great way to help students develop social skills, self-esteem, independence, collaboration, critical thinking, and leadership skills. They can also help students build a healthy personal identity, provide supportive relationships, and encourage goal setting. Apply social-emotional learning frameworks when facilitating after-school programs, and you'll see the positive effect on students down the line.

- **Fairness and transparency.** The classroom can often feel exclusive and unfair to students, especially those who struggle academically. After-school programs provide alternate ways for students to shine, through sports, arts, gaming (including chess), and other outlets. Program leaders or facilitators should always guide students through the rules or expectations of the activities.

- **A concern for wellness.** Effective after-school programs support students' physical and mental health. By providing increased adult supervision, you can help students feel safe, make positive choices, and even avoid risky behaviors. Quality after-school programs should encourage students to find healthy ways to exercise their minds or bodies (Wong, 2008).

- **Accessibility.** Keep an eye out for any barriers to participation, growth, and success. The Afterschool Alliance's 2020 report *America After 3PM* indicates that despite a high *demand* for after-school programs, there's limited *access* to them. For every one child enrolled in a program, there are three waiting to be accepted into one. That means roughly 25 million children can't access after-school support and enrichment, whether due to budget, availability, or transportation restrictions. It's a paradox: After-school programs support working parents and guardians by providing a safe, supportive place to send their children without asking them to pay the high costs of childcare. Yet, these activities aren't always accessible to everyone, and often the children who would benefit most are the ones inadvertently excluded. By designing after-school programs that fit with your student body (in terms of budget, time, and transportation needs), you can increase your impact and reach (Youth.gov, n.d.).

Let's look at some general strategies you might use.

Strategy 1: Take a holistic approach.

When developing or expanding an after-school program, don't focus solely on academics or sports; consider students' whole selves and range of interests and experiences. The emotional, social, and academic needs of students are *all* important.

A holistic approach to facilitating after-school programs includes creating a positive school culture that provides whole-child support for students. These supports must wrap around the children in the program and focus on the academic and nonacademic needs of students. Figure 5.1 illustrates the different components that should be considered when developing holistic after-school programs.

A comprehensive approach allows the school and community to support learning opportunities for students and to engage them in critical thinking activities as well as focus on their emotional well-being. For example, in a variety of after-school contexts (sports teams, gaming groups, academic enrichment sessions, interest-based clubs), you might do any of the following:

- **Teach students how to reflect on their actions and how they impact others in the community.** Students find meaning through connections with their community. Teachers can partner with community and family members, outside organizations, and business officials to provide integrated support and expanded learning opportunities, including after-school and summer programs.

Schools are the hub of communities, bringing together academic, social, and culturally engaging activities.

- **Engage students in applying critical thinking skills to tackle challenges.** Focus on hands-on learning experiences where students work in groups and are encouraged to explore different learning styles. Holistic after-school experiences often include problem-solving exercises and creative projects like photography, gardening, and community banking.

- **Provide opportunities that are personalized to a student's skills and feelings.** Teachers allow students to learn at their own pace in the style that best suits them. Classrooms may be smaller and contain students of different ages and ability levels. At-risk students have a higher chance of success when they feel safe and nurtured. Teachers can foster strong relationships by responding to students' individual strengths and needs. We can encourage self-confidence when students believe that they belong and have the ability to succeed.

FIGURE 5.1
A Holistic Approach to After-School Programs

Strategy 2: Use after-school programs as an opportunity to establish mentorships.

Extracurricular (EC) activities help participants develop a more positive identity as a student *and* as an individual. Having the opportunity to explore ECs can assist them in finding their passions and developing skills that will help them thrive in college, career, and life. These activities can give them a safe outlet as they navigate their life's challenges and provide a sense of purpose, community, and achievement. They can serve as a safe and productive space to be when they are not in school. Through EC activities, students learn to work independently and collaboratively, develop problem-solving skills, and gain a sense of accomplishment. They also build social and emotional skills, making friends and connections that can last a lifetime (DeAngelis, 2001).

The Search Institute has found that students who have a relationship with one caring adult outside the home, often a teacher or mentor at school, are more likely to be engaged and succeed academically (Klein, 2019). According to the Paso del Norte Health Foundation, children with caring adults in their lives are less likely to be bullies *and* less likely to be bullied. They have stronger relationships with their peers and are more involved in after-school activities. Because of this, they have a decreased chance of drug and alcohol use and are more likely to graduate from high school and college. It is safe to say that in today's world, caring adults, teachers, and mentors are critical to a student's success in school and life. Strong adult-child relationships, stability, predictability, and reliability are all protective factors for kids.

Effective after-school programs should facilitate these outcomes, helping students to identify their skills and strengths, increase their confidence, learn to face and overcome challenges, embrace their inner leadership skills, and explore both working together and being independent. It can be so valuable for students to make connections and form friendships outside the peer groups they associate with during the normal school day. These connections and peer interactions should be supervised a little more closely in after-school programs than on the playground and in the lunchroom. This allows for safer structured time and community building.

Strategy 3: Build community experiences inside and outside the school day.

We aren't *just* our students' teachers, and they aren't *just* our students. We're all fellow members of the same community.

Whenever a student of mine would see me in at the supermarket, in the mall, or somewhere else that wasn't school, their face would light up, they'd yell my name, and they'd drag their entire family over to say hello. And when I saw that student in class the next day, I could sense a new feeling of closeness. I learned to leverage this to make new connection pathways. Next time you encounter a student "in the wild," remember what a great opportunity it is to take a step forward in your relationship with that student.

It's often joked that students forget teachers exist outside the classroom. When they see us out in public, it shifts their reality in a constructive way! But we don't need to wait for accidental run-ins to make this shift. We can say hello to our students in the lunchroom, hallways, and outside school. We can support them in their after-school programs and extracurricular activities as well. Even if our own busy lives limit our ability to attend events, we can ask how their game, performance, or competition went. We can ask what book they're reading or what game they're playing at home. Through curiosity about our students' lives outside school, we can recognize and uplift them as fellow members of our community.

There are all kinds of creative in-school methods for fellowship and sharing that teachers can develop. One I've seen talked about is eating lunch with students. It's true that relationships, community, and connections that develop during a "lunch bunch" can be really profound. Of course, time is so valuable to teachers. Many are overworked and really tired... and they need their lunchtime and planning time! I encourage both my fellow administrators as well as district leaders to work on being better at protecting teachers' time. Still, I have seen teachers find effective ways to budget a small amount of time (one day a week or one day a month) to have lunch with students. Some create smaller lunch groups and eat at certain tables on a schedule: this week, it might be the Red table's turn to eat lunch with the teacher; next week, it will be the Blue table's turn; and so on. School leaders can and should do this as well. But be careful not to present lunch with a teacher or leader as a reward earned through attendance or academic performance; it should be something every student gets to do, because we're all part of the community.

Engaging with the Surrounding Community

We have looked at the community within a classroom and school; now let's look at the community surrounding a school. As teachers and administrators, it is important to engage with that community to cultivate a safer, more supportive, and more successful learning environment for our students. By embracing the people our students have at home and in the neighborhoods, we can bridge the gap between school life and home life. We can help build relationships between families, schools, and communities that are *necessary* for student success. A strong connection among home, school, and the greater community helps create an atmosphere of trust—one where parents feel comfortable communicating their needs, responding to feedback, and advocating for their children's education (Kelty & Wakabayashi, 2020).

Engaging with the community reinforces a sense of security among parents and students alike. These outcomes can be felt *and* seen, as this engagement creates opportunities for increased collaboration on educational initiatives. By *consistently* engaging with community members, we can create awareness of the support and resources needed to support our children. Awareness leads to *access*. Engagement leads to *action*. By facilitating awareness and engagement, we can increase access to resources and more effectively address issues like bullying and school safety. By working together, we can hear parents' concerns, and they can hear ours. And finally? We can work together to benefit *everyone* involved in our educational system.

If community engagement feels like yet another task on your to-do list, know that it's not. Its value makes it special. Community engagement is an *investment*. As we know, the whole is always greater than the sum of its parts; we can go even farther if we go together. With the community's support, you won't have to feel like you're carrying the weight of the future generation on your shoulders. The success of the future generation is a *community* effort. Embrace this!

What Is "Good Community Engagement"?

Good community engagement is a two-way process where people in the school and people outside the school come together to create better opportunities for students. It involves a collaborative effort among teachers, administrators, students, parents, local businesses and organizations, and other educational system stakeholders.

To define what *good* community engagement looks like, we can also define what *bad* community engagement looks like. Figure 5.2 compares *good* and *bad* examples of attempts at community engagement.

FIGURE 5.2

"Good" Versus "Bad" Community Engagement

Good Community Engagement	Bad Community Engagement
Mutually Beneficial	One-sided
Focused on Listening	Focused on Complaining
Provides Resources	Takes from Others
Consistent Communication	Announcements with Little Feedback
Inclusive Activities	Exclusionary Practices
Effective Partnership	Poor Relationships

Good community engagement focuses on mutually beneficial outcomes. *Bad* community engagement is a one-sided conversation. It's complaining to parents and organizations about what they're not doing. It's aimed at convincing others to give the school something. *Good* community engagement has different aims and takes a different form. It's spreading awareness of current challenges and issues affecting students, schools, and the community. It's providing resources to show how and why the community can get involved. It's an invitation, not just a demand. It's a group effort. Engaging with the community is about sharing your perspective *and* listening to others. It's seeking to be understood *and* to understand the needs and concerns of the community. Good community engagement is meant to ensure that students have a safe and supportive environment and that parents and community members are able to take advantage of the valuable resources the school offers. It's a way to restore the trust in the school system that many have lost and is so sorely needed.

Community engagement can take on many forms, whether student internships, projects, field trips, forums, fundraisers, surveys, or events. Regardless of our methods, we should focus on the desired outcomes for our students, staff, and community at large. By clarifying the purpose of these collaborations, we can focus on what truly matters. We can channel our efforts, focus our energy, and make a lasting difference in our communities.

Why a Holistic Approach Is Best

Schools and communities should not be seen as separate, opposing groups. We're all connected! Every school stakeholder, whether a student, teacher, administrator, staff member, or parent, is part of the community. When schools and communities unite in their efforts to support the upcoming generation, students achieve higher grades and qualifications. Their attendance goes up. There's less bullying and harmful behavior.

Establishing strong ties between home and school is key to creating a healthy atmosphere that encourages *lifetime* success rather than just immediate achievement. This means supporting our students and their families in the community at all times, not just during special occasions and events.

Some of the happier occasions we can find to connect with students outside school are attending sporting and social events and church services. Funeral services are the most difficult and emotionally draining occasion. As a teacher and principal for nearly 40 years in the inner city, I have attended many funerals—some for students' family members and some for students themselves. The latter have been the saddest days of my career. Nothing can prepare you to lose a young person from your school, to walk into a classroom and see the empty chair that child will never sit in again. There is a permanent void where potential used to be. When tragedy strikes our communities, our perspective shifts. Many of us come to value our work even more. For me, it has meant that I *never* regret the extra effort I spend supporting, engaging, and connecting with our kids and their community.

The Oakland Unified School District (OUSD) is a great example of the school and community uniting. Back in 2010, nearly one-third of this California school district's population were immigrants and refugees. The trauma and challenges students faced were affecting the district and community at large. But they made a difference by developing community-school engagement programs, like student and parent after-school language programs. In fact, Oakland International Academy ended up having the highest graduation rate in the area, at 72 percent. Just over half of the students took college-prep classes to prepare for the future (Positive Action, 2023). OUSD could have washed their hands and chosen to leave these students and their families behind. They could have punished the students for underperforming.

But they helped them instead.

Even more, they realized it was a *community* effort, not just a school one. They sought to help not only students but their *parents* transition to life in the United States. Building relationships with parents and families is essential for creating a supportive and safe learning environment for students. These relationships help create trust between parents, students, teachers, administrators, and the greater community. By regularly engaging with the community, we can discover insight into how to best serve those within it. We can begin to understand the unique circumstances many families face, allowing us to address them individually rather than applying blanket solutions. Effective communication turns school leaders and parents into *partners*. And when parents are engaged, their children are encouraged to engage.

Strategies for Community Engagement

So . . . how do you get started with this work?

A great first step to engaging with the community is learning how students navigate their environments. Many children lead amazing and exciting lives outside school. Sometimes they are involved in interesting activities through their churches, mosques, and synagogues. They participate in community sports, dance, or other arts programs. Educators sometimes learn about these community programs when they're asked to write letters of recommendation for students who are interested in participating. Familiarizing yourself with these aspects of your students' lives can be very rewarding. Students who get regular, committed support in the various spheres of their lives—school, home, and community—often strive to do their best in all three, which is a win-win-win! The students see and feel their "village" at work for their benefit, and they understand that school is a part of that village. On the other hand, if school approval for outside program enrollment is held over the student's head as a threat, the village is under threat as well.

Each year at school, we provide a toy giveaway for our students right before the winter break. We seek the support of our staff, board members, parents, and community to help us provide a gift for any kid who needs one in our school. Honestly, most of the gifts are modest and come from Five and Below, Target, and Walmart, but the kids don't care; it is the kindness that matters most to them. Several years ago, one of my young teachers suggested that I utilize Amazon to help with the toy drive, and she showed me how to set up an Amazon registry. This made it easier for people to donate and ship gifts to us at school. Learning all these new strategies from young teachers was a struggle for me, but I try to practice what I preach (*Be curious! Embrace challenge!*), so I learned how to navigate Amazon. And it has alleviated much extra work and stress for us during the toy giveaway time.

The Amazon project and connecting with the community would be a nice way to end this story, but something more profound happened after I embraced the idea. This successful project gave me the confidence to undertake an even more ambitious outreach to the community. For years, I have been providing school uniforms to students and families in need. Still, I struggled with a proper place to store the uniforms. I had been using an old closet in the school, a musty, crowded space that didn't allow for much organization and couldn't keep the uniforms neat. The success of the toy drive compelled me to think bigger, and I reached out to California Closets, a national custom closet and storage company, to get an estimate on rebuilding our closet with some shelving for uniforms. The California Closets representative came to the school and measured our closet space. She estimated it would cost $10,000 for the closet to be transformed, but she said she would contact us with an official quote. Not unreasonable, but as we were an inner-city school, I had been hoping for a discount!

The representative called us back in a week or so, and I thought she was calling with the definitive quote. She surprised me by saying the company had decided to cover the entire renovation cost. In shock, I asked her to repeat that, and she did, adding that they would throw in a built-in, fold-up ironing board. Yes, we wash and iron for our students, too, and recently won a grant from Whirlpool that covered a new washer and dryer and one year's worth of laundry detergent (almost as expensive as a washer). The new clothes closet, washer, and dryer have been a blessing to our school, students, and families. The community surely made our year.

As educational leaders, we must do everything we can to facilitate the unification of our kids' entire village. It's not the school *versus* the community; it's the school *and* the community. You'll notice that theme running through the positive engagement strategies that follow.

Strategy 1: Join efforts with existing organizations in your community.

There are fellow organizations, businesses, and groups within your district with the same goals as you. Whether it's to empower education, improve community health, or foster creativity, find these communities whose goals align with yours. Find ways you can collaborate and unite your efforts. By working with local families, businesses, or organizations to develop programs or services to meet the needs of our students—such as providing internships, career exploration opportunities, or after-school programs—we can ensure that our youth have access to resources they might not have otherwise been aware of. Apprenticeships and internships are an effective method for students to gain work experience while learning about various career options. Creating hands-on experiences for students can inspire them to become entrepreneurs and contribute to their communities.

Strategy 2: Plan community-driven events and opportunities.

Here are just a few ideas you might try:

- Host speaking events and make them open to the public. Invite teachers, staff, and community members to be the guest speakers.
- Create and send out surveys to identify the issues that most concern parents and community members.

- Host panels to address important topics that concern parents and community members, whether it is school safety, cyberbullying, or mental health.
- Develop peer mentorship programs for students to build connections and leadership skills.
- Host open houses at school for local businesses and leaders to show them all the good things going on in your school. Leadership days, student performances, and learning about the history of your school are all beneficial.
- Take students on field trips to visit local businesses and organizations. This is a great way to expose kids to what working life is (or could be) and bring them into contact with positive role models in the community.

Strategy 3: Participate in established local events.

Attend local festivals, fairs, and shows that bring together members of the public who are interested in education and learning. While you are there, take note of the local businesses and organizations on the sponsor list. Supporting these entities can expand the school's network and potentially provide students with new opportunities and support. Partnering with nonprofits like Habitat for Humanity and Junior Achievement has been invaluable for our students and their families.

Strategy 4: Catalog and share community resources.

Consider creating a list of community resources and partnerships for parents and families. Provide information and education on important issues, news, and initiatives. Transparency is the key to trust. It's how you show the community you're aware of issues they might be facing and doing everything you can to help.

The truth is, to serve our children best, we all must work together. We must work *with* the community to ensure students have access to the resources they deserve. By joining forces, creating opportunities, providing resources, attending local events, and engaging in transparent dialogue, we can create a strong village where our youth feel supported and empowered. Through collaboration between school districts and their communities, educational leaders can ensure every student has access to opportunities for growth inside *and* outside the classroom. Together, we can bridge gaps between home and school to help foster an atmosphere of trust and support within each student's learning journey.

Developing a strong village for all children will be the key to bringing optimism and hope to the community—a village that cares and feels positive with lots of love and support for students, teachers, and staff. The future of our community, our children, and our youth is in everyone's best interest. Let's bring our village together and do everything we can to show our students everything they *can be* and *will be.*

Reflect & Take Action

As teachers and educational leaders in our communities, we hold the opportunity and responsibility to advocate for our students in our schools and districts. This requires us to step up, put in the work, and identify the gaps and disparities our unique communities face. After gaining personal awareness, we can then educate our fellow community members on these issues and develop solutions to empower balance, fairness, and equity for all students.

Providing effective after-school programs is a goal everyone can get behind. All educators should want to see equity in education and ensure students are supported and empowered not only during the school day but after school as well. The relationships we develop in these programs will impact students and adults for the remainder of their lives. Engaging with our community will help to ensure that all students have the resources they need. But true justice in education is about more than resources. Equal opportunities and outcomes, school funding, academic support, and social justice in schools are all important, too. Achieving success for all students will require school and community leaders to focus on all of these aspects and more.

Reflection questions

Take a moment to reflect on Chapter 5 and how it applies to your unique district, school, classroom, and students. Consider:

1. What after-school programs does your school/district currently offer?

2. What program might benefit from your passions and skills? If this program doesn't exist, can you help create and facilitate it?

3. How can you be a teacher *and* a mentor to your students?

4. How are your *school* and *classroom* issues also *community* issues?

5. How can you better engage with and involve community members?

Next steps

True change requires action. Empower the bigger picture by working on long-term goals:

- If you are involved in after-school programs, ensure the work and mission are centered around a holistic approach with the desired social, emotional, and academic student outcomes.

- Collaborate with after-school programs in and around your school to ensure alignment with the school and community goals.

- Facilitate community engagement, whether joining efforts with existing communities, planning community-driven events and opportunities, participating in local events, or providing community resources.

- Schools are the natural centers for activity in many neighborhoods. They should be inviting and safe spaces for students. Use the school as a community hub.

6

Educators Who Choose to Stay

If you are reading this book, it means you are committed to being an educator who makes a difference. Let's be honest: no one accepts a teacher's life of being underpaid and often underappreciated without being prepared to travel an interesting and extraordinary path—namely, applying one's gifts to the great work of motivating students to be their best selves. Even so, no one—not the federal government, the state system, or any school district—should take advantage of those who want to serve in our noble profession by suppressing the passion and gifts we bring as educators. It is time that teachers be allowed to teach in the true sense, the *full* sense. This means helping students master important content and build necessary skills and understanding, but it also means bringing in our own creativity and strengthening relationships with students. The mission of teaching is a rich and fulfilling one, fueled by the heart. It's important to remember this.

I commend you for choosing the life of an educator and attempting to bring the spirit of service and love into your school each day. I wrote this book because I wanted to help you avoid my early career mistakes, which were driven by various constraints—ones placed on me by the system, ones I placed on my students, and my own unexamined biases. I also wanted to reignite the passion of educators who have been in this profession for years and need a revival, a rejuvenation, and a reminder of why they chose to be teachers.

Our students and teachers need emotionally intelligent school and district leaders who value relationships, listening to others, the feelings of all community members, and cultivating an inclusive environment. Today's leaders must invest time, resources, and strategic planning to focus on bringing the joy back to our schools and boosting the learning there. Students need us to fight for a more adaptable system for them—one that will support them and help them thrive, regardless of their race, religion, or economic background. As Paulo Freire (2018) put it, "the solution is not to 'integrate' the oppressed into the structure of oppression, but to transform that structure so that they can become 'beings for themselves'" (p. 74). Students need equity-focused leaders and teachers who embrace a whole-school approach to whole-child development, which maximizes opportunities for all children to succeed. It's time for us to become crazy about our kids and curious about their lives outside school. It's time for us to be consistent adults in our students' lives and to cultivate a culture of love, support, and high expectations!

Why Are Teachers Leaving the Profession?

Early in my career, I took a position as a lead teacher in my inner-city middle school's in-school suspension program. My principal approached me during the first week of school, explaining that the young teacher in charge had quit suddenly and he needed me to take over the class until a replacement or a substitute could be found.

Teachers quitting at our school wasn't a new phenomenon, but teachers leaving during the first week was rare. I did my best to get the class off to a good start, and I tried to reassure the students that their teacher quitting did not mean they were undeserving of a good education. The following week, this teacher stopped in to clean out her desk and closet and grab some personal belongings. Before she left the room, I asked how she was doing and what caused her to leave so abruptly. She began explaining that she'd hurt her ankle in an accident at home before going on for about five minutes about how difficult her first few days on the job had been. The students didn't listen to her, and she didn't feel like she could teach them.

I believed that she had hurt her ankle, and that this injury was a factor in her leaving, but it was also clear that her poor relationship with the students was a bigger factor. It made me sad.

There is no doubt that teaching is a demanding job. I have been working in education since 1987, and even back then, the system put teachers in a vulnerable position. It did not focus on developing trauma-informed teachers and leaders, building resilient or equity-focused educators, or creating cultures of literacy or positive and supportive school cultures. The simple truth is that if we intervene on behalf of just one student in *any* of those areas, we can fundamentally shift the trajectory of their entire life. This is why I wrote my first book *I Choose to Stay* (Thomas-EL, 2003). Back then, I knew that teachers and the rest of the world needed to know that staying in teaching is a choice that every teacher makes. An important and courageous choice.

It's no secret that teachers are leaving the profession in droves. A 2023 McKinsey research report revealed that nearly one in three K–12 teachers in the United States have plans to leave the profession (Bryant et al., 2023). Now, I'm not here to criticize these teachers; staying in the profession even for a year is evidence of hard work. I'm here to reprimand the *system*. A system that has led a *record-breaking* number of educators to quit their jobs. A system that has let educators down instead of building them up. A system that doesn't always support the teachers, mentors, and advocates of the next generation.

There isn't just *one* reason teachers are leaving. The McKinsey report identified a whole list of factors:

1. **Insufficient compensation.** Money is the number one reason teachers either left or plan to leave. Three in four educators who gave this answer indicated that they put more effort into their job than the compensation received in return. Sixty-five percent reported that they simply can't live comfortably on their low salaries. Although teachers are responsible for shaping the minds of the next generation, many are paid less than other professionals with similar education and experience. This can escalate burnout, as teachers struggle to make ends meet while also trying to provide the best possible education to their students.

2. **Unrealistic expectations.** Teachers are overworked and overwhelmed. They feel the weight of all that they are charged to do and don't have the support they need to continue carrying it on their own. These expectations accumulate in the hearts and minds of teachers, and it's beyond frustrating not to have the resources necessary to meet them. The constant criticism and scrutiny placed on teachers can take a toll on their mental health, and many feel like they are not given the respect or recognition they deserve.

3. **Compromised well-being.** When teachers aren't getting the pay and benefits they need, the financial stress can then lead to physical, mental, and emotional stress. Managing unrealistic expectations without the necessary resources can negatively affect their lives outside work. The National Education Association reports that teachers are more likely to have poor *emotional well-being*—defined as job-related stress, burnout, depression, and anxiety—than other professionals (Walker, 2022b).

4. **Poor leadership.** School and district leaders can help combat the challenges—or worsen them. Roughly 30 percent of educators who left or plan to leave do so because of poor leadership. Ineffective leaders fail to recognize the importance of teachers' well-being. They don't provide the resources necessary to promote work-life balance. They place unrealistic expectations on teachers without providing the means to reach these goals.

I suspect the core reason teachers leave teaching is this lack of support and resources. So often they are pressured to do more with less, and it's common for them to be asked to teach classes that are unreasonably large or to work with outdated materials and technology. To support our students, we must support our teachers.

Why It's So Important That Teachers Choose to Stay

A teacher's impact is hard to quantify. Some estimate that the average teacher has an effect on more than 3,000 students' lives (Tornio, 2019). Of course, this number can vary depending on grade level, the length of the teacher's career, and the size of the school. But when you think about it, isn't affecting *one* life impressive and important? When a kind, committed teacher changes just a single student's life for the better, it creates a ripple effect. *That* student can influence their friends, family, and community. *That* experience can guide the student on a path that empowers *them* to make an impact. Like I did, they might even become teachers and principals themselves.

A teacher's value, then, is also immeasurable. It's endless. Teachers help students master academic content and acquire all kinds of skills and understandings. They also help students through everyday challenges of being a kid and teen. They are mentors, role models, and a support system, especially for young people who don't have people at home or in the neighborhood to fill these needs. Teachers who are consistent in their efforts provide a connection and relationship that can redirect students' life paths. Simply by showing up and being there, you can provide a sense of stability many children don't have in their homes and families. You can encourage these same vulnerable kids to believe in themselves, set goals, and follow their dreams.

Teachers, you might not feel this now. You might not see this impact right away. But it's *real*. An astonishing 87 percent of people wish they could go back and tell their teachers how much they impacted their lives (Tornio, 2019). Teachers help pave the way to a better future. They show students opportunities. They show them how to use education to create a better life for themselves. In a confusing, often scary world, teachers simplify the complex and put power back into students' hands. Teachers help students develop the productivity, creativity, and critical thinking they will need in their future studies and in the workplace. And they inspire safety, confidence, and support in children *today*. Teachers aren't just important for the future; they're important *now*.

What Teachers Need

Everything I share in this book ties back to why teachers choose to stay, a topic also addressed in the McKinsey report mentioned earlier (Bryant et al., 2023). I want to highlight these two factors in particular:

1. **Meaningful work.** Over half of the educators who choose to stay report doing so because of the meaning they find in their work.

When we focus less on having "perfect" students and generating "perfect" test scores, educators can focus more on creating engaging, challenging, and joyful classrooms; maintaining significant relationships with our students; creating cultures of literacy; and fostering growth mindsets and resilience. These are the metrics that truly matter.

2. **Colleagues and community.** Both are in the top five reasons teachers stay. Relationships matter—both the ones educators have with our students and the ones we have with *one another*. Community engagement in school can't be a secondary item on your checklist. Collaboration isn't just a chore. Both of these are *tools* and resources that remind us we don't have to do this alone and that there are people who support us, our goals, and our dreams.

In short, teachers leave when they aren't getting what they want and need: a positive and uplifting school with great leaders and strong community. They choose to stay when they work in schools that provide a joyful experience and family atmosphere (see Figure 6.1).

FIGURE 6.1
Why Teachers Leave and Remain in the Profession

Reasons to Leave	Reasons to Stay
• Low Salary/Compensation	• Meaningful Work
• Unrealistic Expectations	• Colleagues and Community
• A Lack of Emotional Well-Being	• Positive School Culture
• Poor Leadership	• Strong Leadership

Even in high-needs schools that serve struggling communities and families, teachers will choose to stay when they feel empowered, appreciated, and supported. Note, too, that good resource availability, high but reasonable expectations, and good work-life balance—the inverse of teachers' reasons to leave—encourage many to stay.

Strategies for Choosing to Stay

So much comes down to the *culture* of the school. When we're crazy about our kids, we get our priorities in check. When we're curious about their lives outside school, we connect with the community. When we're a consistent presence in their lives, we're reminded of how meaningful our work is. When we create cultures of love, support, and high expectations, everyone—ourselves included—feels like they belong. Prioritizing the building of positive relationships will do so much to create the conditions under which educators will choose to stay.

Here are some targeted strategies I recommend for achieving these ends. The first three are more likely to be implemented by school leaders than by classroom teachers, but all faculty and staff should be aware of them and be prepared to take part.

Strategy 1: Make education a team effort.

While teachers can change the course of a student's life, teachers are simply *people*. Each one has a life outside school. They are parents, partners, sons, daughters, brothers, sisters, and *individuals*. They need a support team. A village. Teachers need *other* teachers. They need leaders and administrators who understand, advocate, and provide for their needs. They need the support and involvement of their community. They need the attention, trust, and respect of their students. They need to see themselves as members of a team and partners in education, with shared goals that can be reached through collaboration and mutual support.

Here are some ideas to try:

- **Look for allies.** Find educators in your school or district and even on social media who you can share ideas and strategies with. There are also support groups and communities online to foster teacher collaboration. Just be sure to join communities that are positive and supportive; there are some out there that can be toxic and drain your positive energy.
- **Collaborate on action.** Once you've built meaningful relationships with colleagues, look for ways to support one another by sharing classroom management strategies and tips for effective use of

technology. You might also explore group lesson planning and coordinated family outreach.

- **Ask for help when you need it**. Remember, this is a team effort, and teammates support each other in working toward a common goal. Asking for help teaches you where to turn for the best support, and it establishes you as a learner committed to improvement.
- **Celebrate the success of others.** Gratitude is a great way to lift your attitude.

What I've seen throughout my long career is that when teams of teachers work together, teaching is less stressful, and joyful cultures are more likely to develop. Students and staff become more resilient and benefit from this joy. Collaboration also promotes professional growth throughout a faculty, as educators at all levels and ranges of experience share ideas and strategies and promote one another's development. Teachers deserve to be on amazing teams that value their voices and leadership. Leaders must focus on developing both professional relationships and true collaboration.

Strategy 2: For every expectation placed, provide an equivalent resource.

Teaching is often an underappreciated job, but it is also one of the most *important* professions in the world. We must give educators the resources they need to be effective in the classroom. This includes providing them with up-to-date textbooks, technology, and other materials, as well as funding for professional development opportunities. It is also imperative that we provide the support they need to navigate the emotional and mental stresses of the job through counseling services or other mental health resources. It's all about balance: giving teachers the autonomy they need to lead their students while providing support, collaboration, and teamwork so they don't have to do it alone.

Finally, teachers' hard work and dedication must be recognized through incentives and pay for additional work and public acknowledgment of their contributions to our communities. By showing specific, consistent appreciation, we can help them stay connected to the meaning and purpose behind their careers. Here are some things we do at my school:

- We write grants and apply for funding from state and federal education agencies to fund teacher projects and provide incentives for their hard work.
- Our school has a board of directors at school that are very supportive and recognize the importance of celebrating our teachers and staff. They sponsor various holiday celebrations to lift teachers' spirits and support our prize funds when we do teacher "pick-me-ups" or staff scavenger hunts.
- We partner with other schools to share resources and professional development strategies, along with books and curriculum planning resources.
- We have collaborated with state agencies to provide mental health counseling and support for staff. We have also hosted "pampering days" for staff, during which they can get a professional massage in the staff lounge or a relaxing cup of coffee and breakfast. We have even taken an all-staff trip to the beach for team building.
- We celebrate our staff for their years of service and invite board and community members to attend the events.

Strategy 3: Ask teachers what they need.

Don't guess what teachers might need—*ask them!* This is the true key to supporting our teachers. If you're a principal or teacher leader, ask the teachers you work with what they need from their fellow teachers, administrators, and community. Try these ideas:

- **Conduct anonymous surveys, interviews, and polls to continually understand your teachers' needs and how you can provide for them.** Surveys are a great way to find out about the changes your staff would like to see in your school, the areas they believe you and the district are strong in, and where you need growth. When staff understand that their leaders value their opinion and feedback, it's possible to develop more meaningful relationships. A variety of people should read teacher surveys, including school administrators, district leaders, board members, and parents.
- **Don't punish critical feedback; take it to heart and *act on it*.** Often, the feedback from teachers can be eye-opening, and

sometimes it can be upsetting. I've learned that once you get through the initial pain, you can almost always see the truth of what teachers and staff are feeling. Don't waste time and energy trying to figure out who said "negative" things; instead, look for patterns or frequent comments. These will direct you to the critical areas. Create a plan and then implement some immediate and long-term changes based on the feedback. When we take action that's grounded in teachers' needs, hopes, and priorities, we usually tend to not only solve pressing problems but to build the kind of trust that supports future problem solving.

- **Use the feedback to grow as an administrator and leader, and to inform your district-level leaders about their impact.** Share the results of the survey with someone you trust, like other administrators, your mentor, or even a teacher leader. These are all people who can give you honest and authentic feedback on the results and how you can use them to improve your practice and leadership. Getting feedback from your staff or other administrators is not easy, but the growth that comes from it is worth the pain. Teachers love working for administrators who are supportive, listen, and are willing to learn. This might very well be one good reason they choose to stay.

A side story: My first year as an elementary principal was filled with happy days and excitement. I looked forward to arriving at school each day and to visiting classrooms to see our amazing teachers and students learning and embracing their challenges. But there were also a few teachers who were struggling. One was a 2nd grade teacher who had been at the school a few years before I arrived. I'll call him James. He often complained to me that the students would not listen to or respect him. I could clearly see he cared, but he struggled to make any real connections with the students. At the end of the school year, James came to me and said he was at a crossroads. He wanted to stay because he needed a job, but he wasn't sure if his heart was in teaching. I appreciated his honesty and expressed that I did not want to put him out of a job. Still, James needed to follow his heart and find a job where he could make a true impact on kids. This was hard for me to do because I could tell he loved kids, but I knew he needed to find a different role. That year was his last year at our school.

Several years later, I received a letter at school from James's wife. I was afraid to open it because I was sure it was a note to express how I had ruined his life by encouraging him to leave teaching. Then my secretary jokingly said, "Open it—it might be a thank-you letter." (School secretaries are so amazing: she was right.) The ex-teacher's wife wrote to me to say that her husband was working in a new area, counseling teens who had mental health issues. For the first time, James felt like he was truly making a positive impact on the lives of young people. She said if I had not had an honest conversation with him, he might have continued to pursue teaching and been frustrated for life. He chose not to stay, and that was the right choice.

I once believed that I had to stay in teaching, no matter what. I would not quit, because I thought I *could not* quit—not if I wanted to help kids, which I knew I did. But once I became a school leader, I came to understand that every teacher must intentionally and consistently *choose impact over compliance*. To stay and be happy with staying, to choose this profession, each of us must think about the good we're doing for kids and whether we're able to be as effective as they need us to be. Yes, James did leave the school and teaching profession, but that was where his passion and calling took him. That was the path he needed to take, and he knew why he was on it. This takes us to our final strategy.

Strategy 4: Know and lean on your "why."

This strategy is for every educator: school and district leaders, classroom teachers, paraprofessionals, classified staff, and even school volunteers. When you continually find meaning in your work, making the choice to stay is *more* than worth it. But sometimes you need reminders. Here are some ideas:

- **Develop a positive slogan or mantra you use daily or weekly.** Teachers and educators have faced some very challenging times over the years, and it can be a fight to stay mindful of the greater love and purpose behind what we do. One way some teachers have overcome this struggle is by developing slogans or mantras that they repeat daily or weekly. These are touchstones, reminders of their *why*. I work with teachers who often remind themselves that they inspire students, help them succeed in school, and provide for their families.

- **Build trust with colleagues and students.** Honesty and vulnerability are the key to trusting relationships, and school leaders should be modeling these qualities. This might manifest as owning one's mistakes and asking for help, establishing and following "safe space" guidelines for honest conversation and feedback, and encouraging others to do the same. Educators can build and sustain trusting relationships with *one another* by collaborating in planning sessions, coordinating class trips and group projects, showing mutual respect, and engaging in self-reflection. They can build the same level of trust with *their leaders and administrators* when they place students at the center of their work, come to school prepared and with a positive mindset, model dependability and integrity, and remain open to feedback and advice. Building trust with *students* is the key to an engaging and joyful classroom. In healthy and positive relationships, trust is both the engine and the transmission. Students need educators to listen to and get to know them, and they need to feel safe and supported in every classroom. If we can support them where they are, we can help to take them to where they need to go.

- **Spread the love and joy.** Each of us has a story about why we chose to teach (and why we choose to stay). Share these stories in meetings with parents and colleagues. Write blogs or social media posts about the joys of teaching. When you spread the love and the joy of your *why*, you give those outside the school a view into the beauty of why we continue to teach and work with our amazing students. Yes, the work is hard, and the compensation is modest, but it is important work and so needed. I am hoping that spreading the good news, the joy, and the love we have for teaching children will inspire others to join our community of educators. But I also hope to remind those in leadership who don't care for or appreciate teachers enough to mend their ways.

The Power of Purpose

You don't have to be perfect. There's no perfect teacher, and there doesn't need to be. Because when you're crazy about your kids, they feel it. These relationships form, and you make an impact, simply by being there.

What you *do* need is a *why*—a purpose, a reason for being in the classroom. Beginning a school year with this purpose top of mind makes it easier to build connections with students. As these connections deepen through adherence to the Four Cs, you'll find a deeper sense of purpose, too, and it will motivate you to rise above the barriers and challenges, work harder to create positive classrooms and schools, and do the most good.

As you grow crazier about your kids, you'll become more curious about their lives—not just as students but as individuals. As they grow to trust you, you'll be better positioned to become the role model and mentor you may have dreamed of being. When you're curious about your students' lives and a consistent presence for them, they'll see your classroom as a safe space of learning, love, and support. A place where mistakes are opportunities, fear can turn into confidence, and trauma can heal and resolve into resilience. A place where doubt can turn into belief, and dreams can become reality.

Supporting students through trauma awareness, a culture of literacy, meaningful relationships, and ensuring equity will lead to successful school and life experiences for students *and* teachers. I believe all educators want to make an impact—a *powerful* impact. I truly do. But too many believe that the impact comes from improving students' proficiency on paper: increasing test scores, which purport to be a measure of how prepared they will be to navigate next year's content standards and life after school. And it's true that teachers can help students by helping them acquire skills, knowledge, and understanding! But students also exist in the *now*. There is great standalone value in the connections educators make with students on a daily basis, as this is how relationships are built and trust is earned. This is how educators inspire curiosity, resilience, and real learning. This is how we find purpose that sustains us and establish an influence that lasts. This is why we choose to stay.

Too often in the current system, schools focus on enhancing test scores, not relationships. In some parts of the world, teacher effectiveness and student success are based on high-stakes assessments regardless of any other factors. But real success begins with fostering creativity and productive relationships with kids and their families. Cultivating these relationships helps to develop character in our students. Filling their heads with content knowledge is pointless if they do not possess the temperament or self-regulation required to function in society.

I chose to stay (and *keep* choosing to stay) to make an impact on an entire generation of kids, and I hope reading this book will help inspire you to do the same. Twenty-five years ago, I was offered a higher-paying administrative position that would have had me leaving my teaching job in the middle of the school year; I turned it down. For years, I had preached to students that nobody gets into education "for the money" (because what money?), but the fact was, I really could have used the pay bump that administrative position would have provided. But how could I walk away from my students after just one semester? So many of them had fathers who had walked away from them during their young lives, and I wanted to be a Black man they could count on—a father figure and a role model. Of course, I don't write this to discount anyone's reason for leaving their school, position, or the teaching profession. This is simply my story and my reasons.

What are yours?

Reflect & Take Action

As educators, we strive to create a culture of love, support, and high expectations for our students. We must do the same for our fellow professionals, and we need our colleagues, especially those in leadership, to step up. Teachers deserve to feel safe and secure in their roles. This means respecting and celebrating one another's skills, cultures, and backgrounds: our overlapping strengths and our wide-ranging differences. This is especially important for educators of color.

A National Education Association survey found that 62 percent of Black educators and 59 percent of Hispanic/Latino educators are planning to leave the profession (Walker, 2022a). Their need to feel included, recognized, understood, and respected is high! True equity is the fair treatment and advancement of all employees and ensuring access and opportunity for the entire community.

Disparities in school funding, curricular rigor, teaching effectiveness, and leadership capacity by no means represent the entire list of changes needed in our schools. Academic support and after-school programs, access to technology, mental health and counseling services, and SEL programs are important as well. I have attempted to present the research and stories from the front lines that show programs and strategies that impact student learning and well-being the most.

Each and every student is promised an equal education in our system, but that does not happen often enough. There are persistent achievement and opportunity gaps among disadvantaged students, and we must make improving the education we provide for those students our top priority. This starts and ends with creating cultures of joy, resilience, and learning for our teachers, staff, and children. We must bring curiosity and creativity into our classrooms and schools and establish strong relationships that we nurture and sustain for a lifetime. It is then, and only then, that teachers will choose to stay, and we will give every kid what they truly need,

Throughout this book, I have spoken about the Four Cs but more specifically about the significance of curiosity and learning and connection. Our curiosity about others enables us to be lifelong learners and, thus, more effective educators. Choosing to stay is not only about being in the classroom; it's about choosing to stay where you feel you should be in order to live your *why*. For some of us, choosing to stay can mean going into behavioral counseling, or becoming a nurse, or taking up any number of roles that positively influence the world and people around us.

Choosing to be a lifelong learner leads to the path of greatest impact, and curiosity leads to the most impactful choices. I wish you well on your journey to greatness and would ask simply that you devote yourself to embracing learning in the classroom and in life. It is then that you will develop strong relationships, transform lives, and have the greatest impact on the world. And remember, our true impact as educators is not based solely on our ability to teach, but rather our ability to learn and be curious. Go forth and learn. Live. Love. Meet students' needs, and they will succeed.

Reflection questions

Take a moment to reflect on this chapter and how it applies to your unique district, school, classroom, and students. Consider:

1. Why did you become an educator? What makes the work meaningful to you today? Why are you choosing to stay?
2. How have your former and current colleague teachers impacted your life? *Consider sharing your answer with them.*
3. What changes do you wish to see in the education system?
4. How could those changes start with you?

Next steps

True change requires action. Empower the bigger picture by working on long-term goals:

- Partner with your colleagues when planning lessons and activities for the school year. See how you can collaborate to provide support and make one another's jobs a little easier.

- Weave your purpose, your *why*, into your everyday work routine.
- Identify what expectations are required of you (or of your teachers) and if you have the resources to meet each expectation.
- Administrators: Seek feedback from teachers about what they need; *act on that feedback.*
- Teachers: Seek feedback from students about what they need; *act on that feedback.*

Acknowledgments

No author writes a book alone. Behind each are many supporters, influences, and collaborators, plus a team of publication professionals who share the responsibility of bringing a book to life. While I can't personally thank every person who has influenced my life and work, I want to express my gratitude to those who have contributed to the creation of this book. I have also drawn upon the knowledge of countless authors and researchers from around the world, and I want to thank them for lighting the path for me and others.

A special thank you to Genny Ostertag for welcoming me into the ISTE+ASCD and *Educational Leadership* family. To everyone at ASCD Books—especially my editors, Stephanie Bize and Katie Martin: your insight, creativity, and magic made this book happen. A huge shout-out to Allison Scott for having the vision for this book years ago. Thanks, too, to Principal Kafele, for the incredible Foreword and for decades of friendship and brotherhood.

My family, especially my daughters, have consistently inspired my life and my writing. They have given me nothing but love and support over the years. The success of the children in my family and the joy they felt in school each day inspired me to be a better teacher and leader.

To the teachers and administrators who have supported me over the years, especially my Thomas Edison family—my assistant principals, Liz Yates and John Shelton, and the entire staff, student body, and their families: thank you for holding it down in the community and for your unwavering support of every child.

To my co-authors on other books and thought partners over the years—Dr. Joseph Jones and Dr. T. J. Vari, Cathy Hensford, Neil Gordon, Abby French, J. T. Taylor, Starr Sackstein, Jimmy Casas, and many more: thanks for the feedback, collaboration, and dedication that have enriched my work, the Four Cs, and my presentations. It has truly been a labor of love.

To my NASSP, NAESP, NCSC, and DCSN families; my amazing clients and audiences around the world; and all who helped shape my voice as a speaker and presenter: thank you for empowering me to find my voice.

Thank you to Vincenza, Margherita, and the team at V&M Bistro in Wilmington, Delaware, for providing me with time and a (mostly) quiet space to work on this important project.

To my brother George: Your strength and resilience in battling cancer have inspired me throughout the writing of this book. Your unconditional love and sense of humor have humbled and inspired me.

Finally, to everyone whose stories are woven into these pages—my former students, chess players, coaches, teachers, and principals: thanks for enriching my life with your experiences. Your stories are all great examples of inclusion, empowerment, resilience, dedication, and belonging. Neither this book nor I would exist without you.

References

Afterschool Alliance. (2020). *America after 3 PM*. https://afterschoolalliance.org/AA3PM/data/geo/National/overview

Alexander, J. (2019). *Building trauma-sensitive schools: Your guide to creating safe, supportive learning environments for all students*. Brookes.

American University School of Education. (2022, October 13). *Teacher retention: Preventing teacher turnover*. https://soeonline.american.edu/blog/teacher-retention/

American University School of Education. (2021, February 8). *Trauma-informed teaching strategies for your classroom*. https://soeonline.american.edu/blog/trauma-informed-teaching/

Brown, P. (2023, April 7). Exploring before explaining sparks learning. *Edutopia*. https://www.edutopia.org/article/explore-before-explain-elementary-science/

Bryant, J., Ram, S., Scott, D., & Williams, C. (2023, March 2). *K–12 teachers are quitting. What would make them stay? McKinsey Company*. https://www.mckinsey.com/industries/education/our-insights/k-12-teachers-are-quitting-what-would-make-them-stay

Burke Harris, N. (2018). *The deepest well: Healing the long-term effects of childhood adversity*. Houghton Mifflin Harcourt

Casimir, A. E., & Baker, C. N. (2024). *Trauma responsive pedagogy*. Teachers Reading Project (Teachers Reading and Writing Project, Columbia University). Heinemann.

Chatterjee, R. (2019, November 5). CDC: Childhood trauma is a public health issue and we can do more to prevent it. NPR. https://www.npr.org/sections/health-shots/2019/11/05/776550377/cdc-childhood-trauma-is-a-public-health-issue-and-we-can-do-more-prevent-it

Concern Worldwide. (2023, September 5). The benefits of literacy: How literacy helps fight poverty. https://concernusa.org/news/benefits-of-literacy-against-poverty/

Creekmore, M., & Creekmore, N. (2023). *Every connection matters: How to build, maintain, and restore relationships inside the classroom and out.* ASCD.

Darling-Hammond, L., & Cook-Harvey, C. M. (2018). *Educating the whole child: Improving school climate to support student success* (research brief). Learning Policy Institute.

DeAngelis, T. (2001, March). What makes a good after-school program. *American Psychological Association.* https://www.apa.org/monitor/mar01/afterschool

Delamain, C., & Spring, J. (2020). *Teaching critical thinking skills: An introduction for children aged 7–12.* Routledge.

DeWitt, P., & Slade, S. (2014). *School climate change: How do I build a positive environment for learning?* ASCD.

Dickerson, J. T. (2014). *'Cause I ain't got a pencil.* https://www.yourdailypoem.com/listpoem.jsp?poem_id=4777

Dickson, M., & Nickelsen, L. (2022). *The literacy triangle: 50+ impact strategies to integrate reading, discussing, and writing in K–8 classrooms.* Solution Tree.

Dweck, C. S. (2006). *Mindset: The new psychology of success.* Random House.

Farber, M. (2021, June 2). Games can have a powerful impact on learning. *Edutopia.* https://www.edutopia.org/article/games-can-have-powerful-impact-learning/

Ferlazzo, L. (2021, March 21). Eight instructional strategies for promoting critical thinking. *Education Week.* https://www.edweek.org/teaching-learning/opinion-eight-instructional-strategies-for-promoting-critical-thinking/2021/03

Flannery, M. E. (2020, October 26). *Why we need diverse books.* NEA Today. https://nea-today/all-news-articles/why-we-need-diverse-books

Freire, P. (2018). *Pedagogy of the oppressed* (50th anniversary ed.). Bloomsbury Academic.

Gagliardi, N. (2023, January 25). What happens to your body during the fight-or-flight response. *Cleveland Clinic Health Essentials.* https://health.clevelandclinic.org/what-happens-to-your-body-during-the-fight-or-flight-response

Gilmore, B. (2017, February). 10 ways to promote a culture of literacy. *Educational Leadership, 74*(5), 72–76. https://ascd.org/el/articles/10-ways-to-promote-a-culture-of-literacy

Gorski, P. C. (2018). *Reaching and teaching students in poverty: Strategies for erasing the opportunity gap* (2nd ed.). Teachers College Press.

Gruenert, S., & Whitaker, T. (2024). *School culture rewired: Toward a more positive and productive school for all* (2nd ed.). ASCD.

Hammond, Z. (2014). *Culturally responsive teaching and the brain: Promoting authentic engagement and rigor among culturally and linguistically diverse students*. Corwin.

Jaffe, M. (2021). Recommitting to the joyful classroom. *Rethinking Schools*. https://rethinkingschools.org/articles/recommitting-to-the-joyful-classroom/

Kafele, B. K. (2018). *Is my school a better school because I lead it?* ASCD.

Kaufman, L. (2024). *The leader inside: Stories of mentorship to inspire the leader within*. Impress.

Kaufman, T. (n.d.). What is trauma-informed teaching? *Understood.org*. https://www.understood.org/en/articles/what-is-trauma-informed-teaching

Kelty, N. E., & Wakabayashi, T. (2020). Family engagement in schools: Parent, educator, and community perspectives. *Sage Open, 10*(4). https://doi.org/10.1177/2158244020973024

Klein, T. (2019, June 13). Why every student needs caring adults in their life. *Greater Good Magazine*. https://greatergood.berkeley.edu/article/item/why_every_student_needs_caring_adults_in_their_life

Martin, J. (2021). *Chess strategy for beginners: Winning maneuvers to master the fundamentals of chess*. Rockridge.

Martinez, T. O. (2024, April 18). Investing in school libraries and librarians to improve literacy outcomes. Center for American Progress. https://www.americanprogress.org/article/investing-in-school-libraries-and-librarians-to-improve-literacy-outcomes/

Merrill, S. (2017, August 8). High school flexible seating done right. *Edutopia*. https://www.edutopia.org/article/high-school-flexible-seating-done-right/

Minahan, J. (2019, October). Trauma-informed teaching strategies. *Educational Leadership, 77*(2). https://ascd.org/el/articles/trauma-informed-teaching-strategies

Minero, E. (2015, August 4). Flexible seating elevates student engagement. *Edutopia*. https://www.edutopia.org/practice/flexible-classrooms-providing-learning-environment-kids-need

National Conference of State Legislatures. (2021, November 1). *Supporting student success through afterschool programs*. https://www.ncsl.org/education/supporting-student-success-through-afterschool-programs

Positive Action. (2023, September 13). *Six strategies to promote school and community relations: Why they're important and how to improve them*. https://www.positiveaction.net/blog/school-and-community-relations

Reboot Foundation. (2018). *The state of critical thinking in 2020*. https://reboot-foundation.org/the-state-of-critical-thinking/

Reboot Foundation. (2020). *The state of critical thinking.* https://reboot-foundation.org/the-state-of-critical-thinking/

Regis College. (2023). *Child illiteracy in America: Statistics, facts, and resources.* https://online.regiscollege.edu/blog/child-illiteracy/

Riley, H., & Terada, Y. (2019, January 14). *Bringing the science of learning into classrooms.* Edutopia. https://www.edutopia.org/article/bringing-science-learning-classrooms/

Robertson, D., Romero, M., & Warner, J. (2018). *Building resilience in students impacted by adverse childhood experiences: A whole-staff approach.* Corwin.

Sandstrom, H., & Huerta, S. (2013). *The negative effects of instability on child development: A research synthesis* (Publication No. 412899). Urban Institute.

Siegel, D. J., & Bryson, T. P. (2012). *The whole-brain child: 12 revolutionary strategies to nurture your child's developing mind.* Bantam.

Souers, K., with Hall, P. (2016). *Fostering resilient learners: Strategies for creating a trauma-sensitive classroom.* ASCD.

Souers, K. V. M., with Hall, P. (2019). *Relationship, responsibility, and regulation: Trauma-invested practices for fostering resilient learners.* ASCD.

Sparks, S. D. (2019, March 13). Why teacher-student relationships matter. *Education Week.* https://www.edweek.org/teaching-learning/why-teacher-student-relationships-matter/2019/03

Steinberg, M. P., Allensworth, E., & Johnson, D. W. (2011, May). *Student and teacher safety in Chicago Public Schools: The roles of community context and school social organization.* Consortium on Chicago School Research at the University of Chicago. https://consortium.uchicago.edu/publications/student-and-teacher-safety-chicago-public-schools-roles-community-context-and-school

Sutherland, A. (2014, July 29). *How instability affects kids.* Institute for Family Studies. https://ifstudies.org/blog/how-instability-affects-kids

Thomas-EL, S. (2003). *I choose to stay: A Black teacher refuses to desert the inner city.* Kensington.

Tomlinson, C. A. (2014). *The differentiated classroom: Responding to the needs of all learners* (2nd ed.). ASCD.

Tomlinson, C. A. (2023). *Teaching up to reach each student* (Quick Reference Guide). ASCD.

Tornio, S. (2019, May 15). 12 powerful statistics that prove why teachers matter. *We Are Teachers.* https://www.weareteachers.com/teacher-impact-statistics/

Turnbaugh, A. (2015). *The principal's guide to afterschool programs K–8: Extending afterschool learning opportunities.* Skyhorse.

U.S. Environmental Protection Agency. (2012, November). *Student health and academic performance* (Quick Reference Guide). https://www.epa.gov/sites/default/files/2014-08/documents/student_performance_findings.pdf

Venet, A. S. (2021). *Equity-centered trauma-informed education*. W. W. Norton.

Walker, T. (2022a, February 1). Survey: Alarming number of educators may soon leave the profession. *NEA Today*. https://www.nea.org/nea-today/all-news-articles/survey-alarming-number-educators-may-soon-leave-profession

Walker, T. (2022b, June 16). Make educator well-being a priority—Now. *NEA Today*. https://www.nea.org/nea-today/all-news-articles/make-educator-well-being-priority-now

Whitby School. (n.d.). *8 critical thinking skills kids learn at chess camp*. https://www.whitbyschool.org/passionforlearning/8-critical-thinking-skills-kids-learn-at-chess-camp

Wong, A. M. (2008, February 24). The secrets of successful afterschool programs. *Usable Knowledge*. https://www.gse.harvard.edu/ideas/usable-knowledge/08/02/secrets-successful-afterschool-programs

Youth.gov. (n.d.). *Benefits for youth, families, and communities*. https://web.archive.org/web/20241231052710/ https://youth.gov/youth-topics/afterschool-programs/benefits-youth-families-and-communities

Ziegler, B., Ramage, D., Parson, A., & Foster, J. (2022). *Trauma-sensitive school leadership: Building a learning environment to support healing and success*. ASCD.

Index

The letter *f* following a page locator denotes a figure.

accessibility, after-school programs and, 94–95

acknowledgement, importance of, 21, 52–53

adaptive leadership, modeling, 36

after-school events
creating and promoting joyful, 70
showing up for, 24–25, 27, 49

after-school programs
basketball example, 89–90
benefits for students, 97
holistic, 95–96, 96*f*
mentorships with, 97
as opportunities, 91–93

after-school programs, building
accessibility and, 94–95
community partner support, 94–96
concern for wellness in, 94
fairness in, 94
goals and objectives in, 93–94
leadership for, 93
scheduling in, 93

after-school programs, building— (*continued*)
social-emotional development opportunities in, 94
transparency in, 94

bathrooms, maintaining, 19

behavior, modeling and reinforcing positive, 30–31

believe that all children can be successful, 37–38

belonging, creating a sense of, 22

biases, checking your personal, 24

book clubs, 26

books, diversity in, 60–61

boundaries, setting and sticking with, 29–30

building systems, maintaining, 19

caring about students, 22–23, 32–33, 35. *See also* Consistent Adults in Students' Lives

celebrating
the custodial team, 18–19

celebrating—(*continued*)
   progress, 66–67
   stakeholders, 36–37
   success, 115
change, being open to, 36
character-building, critical thinking
   as, 79–80
chess, 4–5, 64, 74–77, 79, 82
classroom design, 69
classrooms
   challenging, 58*f*, 62–67
   engaging, 57–62, 58*f*
   joyful, 58*f*, 67–70
   qualities of engaging, challenging,
     joyful, 56–57
   spending time outside the, 26–27
   trauma-informed practice in,
     51–52
collaboration, fostering a culture of,
   35
colleagues, as reasons educators stay,
   113
communication
   with the community, 36–37
   of expectations, 38
   with families, 20, 22
   focus on positive, 36
   mindful to avoid bias, 24
   prioritizing, 35
   in trauma-informed practice, 43
community
   in after-school programs, 94–96
   communicating with the, 36–37
   creating with students, 98–99
   learning about and getting involved
     in students,' 25–26, 49
   as reasons educators stay, 113
community activities, attending, 49
community partnership examples,
   103–104

community resources, leveraging,
   25–26, 59, 62
community-school engagement
   good, 100–101, 100*f*
   a holistic approach to, 101–102
   purpose in, 99
community-school engagement
  strategies
   community-driven events and
     opportunities, 104–105
   join efforts with existing organiza-
     tions, 104
   participate in established local
     events, 105
   student lives, learn about, 102–103
   toy giveaway, 103
compensation, retention and, 110
competitions, showing up for, 24–25,
   27, 49. *See also* after-school events
confidence building in trauma-informed practice, 43
consequences
   focusing less on, 52
   following through with, 29
consistency, trauma-informed practice
   and, 51–52
Consistent Adults in Students' Lives
   benefits for students, 33–34
   joyful school culture and, 68
   overview, 28–29
Consistent Adults in Students' Lives
  strategies
   be an ongoing, joyful influence,
     32–33
   boundaries, expectations and
     routines, 29–30
   positive behavior and language,
     30–31
   routines, perfecting, 30
co-teaching, 27

Crazy About Kids
    benefits for students, 22
    meaning of, 17–18, 76
Crazy About Kids strategies
    listen and learn, 19–20
    physical space, 18–19
    share your stories, 21–22
    welcome with joy, 21
creativity, 50, 69
critical analysis, modeling, 84
critical thinking
    about, 77–78
    in after-school programs, 96
    for all, 86
    as character-building, 79–80
    in a Four Cs mindset, 86–87
    a success story, 78–79
critical thinking, strategies for
  empowering
    ask for whys and hows, not whats,
        85–86
    creative play, 81–82, 82*f*
    critical analysis, modeling, 84
    decision making, modeling, 84
    instructional approaches, varying,
        84–85
    positive decision-making experi-
        ences, 83
    resources, diversify, 85
    teamwork, 84
critical thinking skills, 50, 76, 96
culture of joy, fostering a, 67–70
culture of literacy, 59–61
Culture of Love, Support, and High
  Expectations
    benefits for students, 38
    overview, 34–35
Culture of Love, Support, and High
  Expectations strategies
    be adaptive and open to change, 36

Culture of Love, Support, and High
  Expectations strategies—(*continued*)
    believe that all children can be
        successful, 37–38
    be visible and engaged, 35
    keep communication lines open,
        36–37
    listen to stakeholders, 36–37
    set high expectations, 37–38
curiosity, encouraging, 69
Curious About Students' Lives Outside
  School
    benefits for students, 27
    importance of, 50
    overview, 22–24
Curious About Students' Lives Outside
  School strategies
    check personal biases, 24
    show up for after-school events,
        24–25
    spend time in school but outside
        the classroom, 26–27
    students' communities, learn about
        and get involved, 25–26
custodial team, celebrate contribu-
    tions of the, 18–19

decision making, modeling, 84
decision-making experiences, positive,
    83
difficulty, normalizing, 66–67
discipline
    focusing less on, 52
    restorative, in trauma-informed
        practice, 43–44

educators
    challenges of, 3
    who leave, reasons of, 109–111, 113*f*,
        117–118

educators who choose to stay
  needs of, 112–113
  purpose, power of, 120–121
  reasons of, 113*f*
  value of, measuring, 111–112
educators who choose to stay, ideas for
  encouraging
  ask for help when needed, 115
  ask teachers what they need,
    116–117
  Black and Hispanic/Latino, 122
  build trust, 119
  celebrate success, 115
  develop a positive slogan or man-
    tra, 118–119
  don't punish feedback, use it to
    grow, 116–117
  know and lean on your why,
    118–119
  make education a team effort,
    114–115
  provide resources for expectations,
    115–116
  spread the love and joy, 119
emotional intelligence, expanding, 36
emotional needs, focus on students,'
  33
emotional regulation, modeling, 31
empathy, 31, 52
engaged, being, 35
engagement, 76–77, 82
expectations, 29–30, 111, 115–116. *See
  also* Culture of Love, Support, and
  High Expectations
explore-before-explain method, 83

fairness in after-school programs, 94
families. *See also* Consistent Adults in
  Students' Lives
  communicating with regularly, 20

families—(*continued*)
  learning about cultural back-
    grounds of, 24
  sharing your story with, 22
feedback, punishing vs. growth from,
  116–117
field trips, 26–27
flip the script, 52–53
Four Cs. *See also specific Cs*
  critical thinking and the, 86–87
  illustrated, 16*f*
  meaning of, 56
  overview, 15–17

games to promote critical thinking,
  81–82, 82*f*
goals and objectives in after-school
  programs, 93–94
greetings, 21
growth, encouraging, 69
growth mindset, 63–64

health and safety, maintaining physical
  spaces for, 18–19
holistic school mindset, adopting a,
  50–51
Hyland, Nah'Shon ("Bones"), 41–42
hypervigilance, 42

intentions, stating to students, 21
interest talk, 20

joy
  in after school events, creating, 70
  focusing on, 52
  fostering a culture of, 67–70
  in learning and teaching, 70
  obstacles to student, 56–57
  and rigor, balancing, 38
  spreading, 119

joy—(*continued*)
    welcome all students with, 21
joyful influence, being an ongoing,
    32–33

kindness, modeling, 31

language, modeling and reinforcing
    positive, 30–31
leadership
    adaptive, 36
    in after-school programs, 93
    retention and, 111
learning
    finding joy in, 70
    importance of ongoing, 36
    obstacles to student, 56–57
    self-directed for understanding
        trauma, 47
    from students, 19–20, 48–49
learning environments in trauma-in-
    formed practice, 51–52
listening
    for healing, 35
    to stakeholders, 36–37
    to students, 19–20, 48–49
literacy, prioritizing, 58–62
literacy plan, developing a, 61–62
love, spreading the, 119. *See also*
    Culture of Love, Support, and High
    Expectations

mantra, developing a positive, 118–119
mentorships with after-school pro-
    grams, 97
mindful communication, biases and,
    24

office hours, 70
ownership, creating, 22

patience
    chess and, 77
    in trauma-informed practice, 52
physical space, maintaining, 18–19
play, promoting critical thinking with,
    81–82, 82*f*
predictability, trauma-informed
    practice and, 51–52
problem solving skills, 50
professional development, 36, 50
progress, celebrating, 66–67
promises, following through with,
    29
purpose, power of, 120–121

relationships. *See also* Consistent
    Adults in Students' Lives
    engaging classrooms and, 58
    focusing on emotional needs, 33
    joyful school culture and, 68
    prioritizing, 35
    supportive and consistent, 28
    in trauma-informed practice, 43,
        48
relationships, developing
    after-school basketball, 89–90
    good student-teacher, 64
    outside the home, benefits of, 97
    in-school suspension program,
        12–14
resilience, 50, 63–64
resources
    diversify to empower critical
        thinking, 85
    providing for each expectation,
        115–116
retention. *See* educators who choose
    to stay
rigor and joy, balancing, 38
role model, being a good, 32

routines, setting and sticking with, 29–30

safety
    focusing on, 52
    maintain physical spaces for, 18–19
scheduling after-school programs, 93
school community, working with the, 49
school culture. *See also* Culture of Love, Support, and High Expectations
    joyful, 68
school events, creating and promoting joyful, 70
schools, challenges faced by, 3–4
security, trauma-informed practice and, 51–52
self-reflection, 24, 47–48
share your stories, 21–22
slogans, developing positive, 118–119
social-emotional development opportunities in after-school programs, 94
social-emotional learning (SEL) programs, 51
sporting events, showing up for, 24–25, 27, 49
sports
    basketball example, 89–90
    field trips for, 26
    joining students in, 27
stakeholders, listen to and celebrate, 36–37
stories
    listen to and learn from students,' 19–20
    share your own, 21–22
struggle, encouraging productive, 66–67

students
    caring about, 22–23, 32–33, 35
    listening to and learning from, 19–20, 48–49
    prioritizing needs, challenges, and goals of, 68–70
students' village, become a part of the, 33, 102–104
success
    celebrating, 115
    obstacles to student, 56–57
suspension, redefining, 52

teaching
    best compensation from, 76, 90
    critical thinking, 77–78
    finding joy in, 70
    varying to empower critical thinking, 84–85
teamwork
    in education, 114–115
    to empower critical thinking, 84
Thomas-EL, Salome
    early career, 11–15, 44–46, 58–59
    in hospital, 1–3
    relationships, meaning of, 90–91
    teaching chess, reasons for, 4–5
time, spending in school but outside the classroom, 26–27
toy giveaway, 103
transparency in after-school programs, 94
transportation talk, 20
trauma
    meaning of, 42–44
    overcoming, Hyland, Nah'Shon ("Bones"), 41–42
trauma-informed practice
    core principles, 43–44, 44*f*
    an educator's responsibility, 44–46

trauma-informed practice—(*continued*)
    methods for increasing under-
      standing, 47–48
trauma-informed practice strategies
    adopt a holistic school mindset,
      50–51
    create a predictable, consistent,
      and secure learning environ-
      ment, 51–52
    flip the script, 52–53
    recognize that students are indi-
      viduals, 48–50
trauma-informed teacher, path to
    becoming a, 47–48

trust
    building as a reason to stay, 119
    establishing, 29–30

visible, being, 35

water fountains, maintaining, 19
weekend events, showing up for,
    24–25, 27, 49
welcome all students with joy, 21
well-being
    in after-school programs, 94
    retention and, 111
    supporting, 18–19

About the Author

Salome Thomas-EL has been a teacher and principal since 1987. He is currently a K–8 principal in Wilmington, Delaware. He received national acclaim as a teacher and chess coach at Vaux Middle School in Philadelphia, where his students won world recognition as eight-time national chess champions. Principal EL is the author of the bestselling books *I Choose to Stay* (movie rights optioned by Disney Films) and *The Immortality of Influence*. He is also the co-author of three other books, *Passionate Leadership, Building a Winning Team*, and *Retention for a Change*. He speaks to groups around the country and has appeared on C-SPAN, CNN, and NPR Radio.

Principal EL earned his undergraduate degree at East Stroudsburg University and trained in leadership at Cheyney University and Lehigh University in Pennsylvania. His graduate studies included work in Cambridge, England. He holds a doctorate in education leadership from Wilmington University in Delaware. Principal EL has received the Marcus A. Foster Award as Philadelphia's Outstanding School District Administrator and the University of Pennsylvania's Martin Luther King Award. *Reader's Digest* recognized Principal EL as an "Inspiring American Icon," and he was once selected as *Philadelphia* magazine's, "Best Philadelphian." He was featured on *Good Morning America* and has appeared on the Oprah Radio Network.

Principal EL lives in Pennsylvania with his family. To learn more about him and his work, visit his website (www.principalel.com) and connect with him on Instagram (dr.principalel), Facebook (Principal EL), and Bluesky (@drprincipalel).

Related ASCD Resources: Meeting Students Needs

At the time of publication, the following resources were available (ASCD stock numbers in parentheses).

Becoming the Educator They Need: Strategies, Mindsets, and Beliefs for Supporting Male Black and Latino Students by Robert Jackson (#119010)

Building a Positive and Supportive Classroom (Quick Reference Guide) by Julie Causton and Kate MacLeod (#QRG120098)

Every Connection Matters: How to Build, Maintain, and Restore Relationships Inside the Classroom and Out by Michael Creekmore and Nita Creekmore (#123010)

Fix Injustice, Not Kids and Other Principles for Transformative Leadership by Paul Gorski and Katy Swalwell (#120012)

Powerful Student Care: Honoring Each Learner as Distinctive and Irreplaceable by Grant Chandler and Kathleen M. Budge (#123009)

Teach for Authentic Engagement by Lauren Porosoff (#123045)

"Teaching Up" to Reach Each Learner (Quick Reference Guide) by Carol Ann Tomlinson (#QRG123035)

Trauma Responsive Educational Practices: Helping Students Cope and Learn by Micere Keels (#122015)

The Way to Inclusion: How Leaders Create Schools Where Every Student Belongs by Julie Causton, Kate MacLeod, Kristie Pretti-Frontczak, Jenna Mancini Rufo, and Paul Gordon (#123001)

We Belong: 50 Strategies to Create Community and Revolutionize Classroom Management by Laurie Barron and Patti Kinney (#122002)

Well-Being in Schools: Three Forces That Will Uplift Your Students in a Volatile World by Andy Hargreaves and Dennis Shirley (#122025)

For up-to-date information about ASCD resources, go to www.ascd.org. You can search the complete archives of *Educational Leadership* at www.ascd.org/el. To contact us, send an email to member@ascd.org or call 1-800-933-2723 or 703-578-9600.

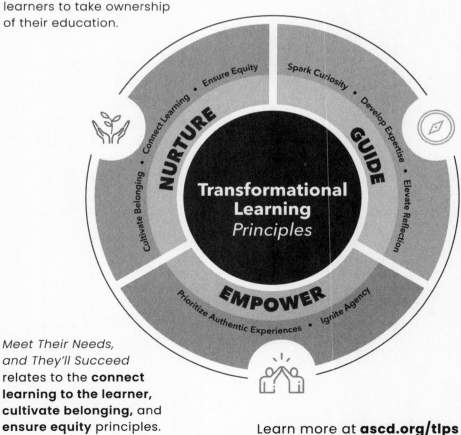

iste+ascd

Transform Instruction to
Transform Students' Lives

Our Transformational Learning Principles (TLPs) are evidence-based practices that ensure students have access to high-impact, joyful learning experiences.

Endorsed by AASA and NASSP, the TLPs provide a shared language and a framework for reimagining teaching and learning, focusing on nurturing student growth, guiding intellectual curiosity, and empowering learners to take ownership of their education.

Connect Learning • Ensure Equity

Spark Curiosity • Develop Expertise

NURTURE

GUIDE

Cultivate Belonging

Elevate Reflection

Transformational Learning *Principles*

EMPOWER

Prioritize Authentic Experiences • Ignite Agency

Meet Their Needs, and They'll Succeed relates to the **connect learning to the learner, cultivate belonging,** and **ensure equity** principles.

Learn more at **ascd.org/tlps**